/99

Punishment
AN ILLUSTRATED HISTORY

PETER N WALKER

Punishment
AN ILLUSTRATED HISTORY

Special Edition for the
Readers Union
Group of Book Clubs

DAVID & CHARLES
NEWTON ABBOT

The mood and temper of the public with regard to the treatment of crime and criminals is one of the most unfailing tests of the civilization of any country.

Winston Churchill, 1910

0 7153 5581 3

© Peter N. Walker 1972
All rights reserved. No part of this
publication may be reproduced, stored
in a retrieval system, or transmitted,
in any form or by any means, electronic,
mechanical, photocopying, recording or
otherwise, without the prior permission
of David & Charles (Publishers) Limited
Set in Times 11/13pt by C. E. Dawkins (Typesetters) Ltd SE1
and printed in Great Britain
by Straker Brothers Ltd., Whitstable
for David & Charles (Publishers) Limited
South Devon House Newton Abbot Devon

Contents

Illustrations

Permission to reproduce illustrations was given as follows:
British Museum: Cover and figs 15, 17, 19, 23, 25, 31, 35, 37, 38, 39,
42, 44, 55, 57, 58, 59, 61, 62
Mansell Collection: Figs 3, 5, 7, 8, 14, 20, 22, 28, 29, 30, 33, 40, 41,
45, 48, 50, 51, 52, 53, 54, 56, 60
Radio Times Hulton Picture Library: Figs 1, 2, 6, 9, 10, 11, 12, 13,
16, 18, 21, 24, 26, 27, 34, 43, 46, 47, 49
Israel Exploration Society: Fig 4
Central Office of Information (Crown Copyright): Figs 63, 64, 65
John Edenbrow: Figs 32, 36

Introduction

To maintain order in any society, however free, a system
of rules and penalties is necessary. Otherwise, anarchy would
result and whilst that may represent freedom to a minority, it
would become a frightening threat to the majority. There are
methods of control in every country, all designed to regulate
the movements of the inhabitants. The same practice extends
to much smaller groups of people, such as social clubs or
business organisations. In each case, a set of rules is fashioned
to govern the routine of the people and if those rules are
broken, punishment is imposed. This can include temporary
or permanent loss of privileges, a fine or even expulsion from
the organisation.

The punishment varies according to the degree of transgression and its objects are two-fold—to prevent a repetition of the offence and to punish the offender, if he is considered fully responsible for his crime. This logic is carried into the criminal world, but of course legal wrongs differ from place to place. What is legal in some countries is illegal in others. Take, for example, adultery: at various times and places throughout history this was punishable by death, but in England today it is a civil wrong carrying no criminal penalty. Exactly what constitutes adultery is very much open to question: the Christian churches teach that all sexual intercourse outside marriage is adultery and in Connecticut, such acts (there known as sinful dalliance) were once punished by making the parties get married! We are told, on the other hand, that an Eskimo considers it courteous to lend his wife to male visitors.

Furthermore, an occurrence can be a crime one day, yet perfectly legal the next. Suicide, for example, is no longer a crime in England, nor are homosexual acts in certain circumstances. Similarly, the constituents of a crime can change with alterations in the law—homicide has been constantly re-defined over the centuries until today we have off-shoots like manslaughter, infanticide, child destruction and even abortion. The punishments for these crimes differ and, indeed, changing social demands can bring about new forms of homicide. A good example is 'causing death by the dangerous driving of a motor vehicle'. This offence carries five years' imprisonment as its maximum penalty.

In addition to serious crimes, there is a multitude of minor anti-social acts which must also be controlled so that society as a whole can function efficiently and live in comfort. For instance, if there were no laws to control the driving, parking

fig 1 Lady Mary Bruce, exposed as a public spectacle, at Roxburgh ▶
Castle by order of Edward I

and construction of motor vehicles, our roads would become choked and unusable. A host of regulations, invariably described as petty, has developed to check hazards while allowing the motorist the maximum possible freedom. Funnily enough, the motorist is the person who objects most strongly to these rules, yet if they did not exist he would not be able to follow his pleasure or his work. Traffic laws are a good illustration of how legal rules and their enforcement are for the benefit of the community at large. Often, an individual may feel that he is unjustly treated or subjected to over-rigid controls, but this is sometimes unavoidable; it is the penalty for living in a society which is growing progressively more complex and therefore must have more rules and regulations.

Men have been compiling laws, written and unwritten, since the beginning of time. Changing values of morality, social requirements, education and sheer numbers of people combine to bring changes in the law. Statutes are updated to meet the growing demands, but in order to be effective, any breach of them, however small, must be met with a 'punishment', a deterrent of some sort.

It is the task of the legislators to devise adequate scales of punishment. These must be wholly effective and just. Fines, probation, imprisonment and even death are used today; but if a fine is too great or too small, imprisonment too long or too short, its objects are defeated. To take the extreme case, death for petty offenders would make life cheap and, as a form of punishment, would lack real value.

Right through history proper punishment of offenders has been a major problem. In early times, savagery and violence were considered ideal deterrents and were regularly meted out; death was commonplace and delivered by an overwhelming number of ingenious methods. For minor offences, degradation was popular; the thinking of the ancients—and, indeed, the not-so-ancients—was that if a villain was to be made to look a fool, the public ought to witness his downfall and

fig 2 Method of punishing the idle in the poor house at Hamburg, by suspending them in a basket over the table where the more industrious are at their meals

misery. Punishment and deterrence were thus combined. It became fashionable to concoct complicated and sadistic penalties. One is shown on p. 16. The head of the victim was pushed through a hole at the twelve o'clock position of a large clock. The hour- and minute-hands were re-set upon each other's axles. As the now short minute-hand ticked around, it nicked the victim's throat, while the hour-hand, now long and keenly sharpened, jerked around slowly and inexorably towards the victim's exposed neck.

But is this any more fiendish than the more recent acts of civilised Englishmen who experiment with 'better' methods of hanging, or Americans who test executions by gas, electricity or shooting?

The purpose of this book is not to expound reasons why punishments are inflicted, nor to justify them, nor to express opinions for or against any specific method. It is simply to record the development of criminal sanctions over the years.

◄ *fig 3* The clock face of Schaumburg—'But still the clock ticked on and brought the blade nearer'

2 In the Beginning
BC 2347 - AD 1200

It is impossible to determine the precise origins of criminal
punishment, but it seems that one of the first sanctions was
the law of 'blood for blood' which was established after the
Great Flood in BC 2347. The Bible of course provides plenty
of information on the punishments of some of the early world.
In BC 1451, Moses commanded the Jews to build cities for
the refuge of manslayers; in BC 1444, a similar order was issued
to Joshua. Rome also became a place of criminal shelter. The
fact that such refuges existed indicates that the criminals must
have been fleeing from something or someone.

The Law of Moses did inflict the death penalty for
blasphemy, and by BC 1179, murder was a capital crime among

fig 4 A crucified man

the Egyptians and Greeks. In that year, too, the Greeks established the Court of the Ephetae to try murderers, a very early example of punishment being inflicted by a *court* as a deterrent against crime. The responsibility usually rested upon a ruler and this court was therefore unique.

Crucifixion was a common penalty employed by the early Jews. They called it 'fastening to a tree'; in BC 1022, the Gibeonites hanged Saul's son from a tree. Crucifixion also existed in ancient China and was used by the Carthaginians,

Phoenicians and the early Assyrians. In Carthage anyone was liable, but the Roman laws stipulated, initially, that only slaves could be crucified. This was later changed, and during Titus' siege of Jerusalem in AD 70 the Romans crucified 500 Jews every day. However, there were insufficient crosses to cope with the demand, and when the supply of wood was exhausted, the purge was brought to an abrupt end. Crucifixion was eventually abolished in AD 325 by Constantine I.

In 1968, the body of a crucified man was unearthed not far from the likely site of Christ's crucifixion. This discovery changed the traditional ideas about the method of crucifixion, for it appears the victim was supported by a narrow shelf on the upright of the cross which carried the weight of the body, while the arms were outstretched and nailed to the wood. The legs, broken below the knees, were twisted to one side and fixed with one nail to the cross at a point just below the supporting bar—a viciously cruel torture (see p. 20).

In the years before Christ, other methods of punishment were practised—the Jews, Persians and other ancient nations favoured live burial, particularly for women who contravened the laws. Xerxes is said to have buried alive nine sons and nine daughters of the Edonians. Xerxes' wife, Amestris, ordered the live burial of fourteen children of high-ranking citizens. The legendary founders of Rome, Romulus and Remus, were the sons of a vestal virgin called Ilia who was compelled to break her vows of chastity; for this transgression, she was buried alive. Other vestal virgins suffered the same death. Opimia in BC 481; Urbinia in BC 470; Misurtia in BC 337; and Sextilia in BC 273. In BC 116, Licinia was buried alive and her accomplice scourged to death for committing incest. The Laws of Nuna later inflicted death by stoning for impure vestal virgins, but Tarquinus Priscus disagreed with this practice; he wanted them buried alive and one of the last to suffer in this way was Cornelia in AD 91. Vestal virgins were abolished in AD 389.

fig 5 The wheel

The ancient Greeks favoured punishment by the wheel. Criminals were bound to the outer rim and whirled around until they died. Seven hundred years before Christ, Draco tried to suppress crime in Greece by imposing capital punishment for *every* offence. This practice could never survive and, inevitably, less severe penalties were introduced, among them the pillory. The Gauls, too, used the pillory, under the name of *boia,* and it became widespread in Europe, where it was popular for minor offences, such as drunkenness. This social problem has been penalised since the beginning of civilisation; in BC 589, the ancient Greeks inflicted one penalty for the actual offence and another for the intemperance which caused it!

In the fifth century before Christ, Servius Tullius, the sixth king of Rome, made the first attempt to distinguish criminal offences from civil wrongs: criminal affairs were to be decided by the king, whilst civil wrongs would be settled by a panel of judges. He retained the death penalty for many offences, particularly murder, treachery and violation of public morals, and for unfortunate vestals who lost their virginity. The example of Servius led to the establishment of a legal code in Rome. Its rules, drawn up by a commission of ten men known as *decemvirs,* were engraved on ten brass tables and became known as the Law of the Ten Tables. Two more rules were added in BC 450 and so the famous Law of Twelve Tables was born. The Tables were destroyed around BC 390 and only fragments of the laws have survived. They included legal procedures, family rights, and civil and criminal laws; basically they were 'poor man's laws', designed to protect the citizen rather than give more power to the ruling classes. For instance, the borrower of money put himself into the power of his creditor; a scale of payments was to be levied against those who broke another's bones or inflicted physical injury; it was wrong to whisper evil incantations; a man who had been robbed could search a suspect's house for the missing goods; false witnesses could be thrown off the cliffs, fire-raisers could be burnt, and those who stole crops at night could be hanged at the site of their crime as a sacrifice to Ceres, the goddess of the harvest.

To cope with illiteracy, the phraseology of the laws was quaint. It was sometimes difficult to comprehend the precise meaning at first reading, eg 'If he summons to law, if he does

not go, he shall call up witnesses. Then he shall seize him. If he evades arrest or resists, he shall lay hands on him.' The laws display a wide variety of penalties and in some circumstances a victim could wreak his own punishment: a thief caught redhanded at night could be killed by his captor, though if caught in the daytime he could suffer such a death only if he used violence to escape. In general, though, the Roman state's assumption of a major role in dealing with offenders has become a model for all civilised societies.

Some odd penalties crept into ancient rules: citizens of Sparta could be whipped if they became too fat; in Rome, the *Lex Julia et Papia Poppaea* imposed a fine on bachelors who did not marry by a specified age. Even earlier, bachelors suffered public ridicule, and by the laws of Lycurgus were branded for infamy!

In England some 450 years before Christ, the early Britons had no written laws, but a primitive method of ensuring conformity existed: malefactors were drowned in quagmires. In some European countries, criminals were placed in wicker baskets built in the shape of an idol, and burnt as a sacrifice to their gods. Gods of all types, including the Christian one, have featured strongly in history's changing penal system.

Some 150 years after Christ's death, the Church introduced the system of penance as atonement for one's sins, and by the fourth century, penitents had been classified in special groups—the weepers, the hearers, the kneelers and the standers. By AD 410, Alaric had captured Rome and ordered that all who took refuge in the churches should be spared. This form of relief from punishment persisted the world over until comparatively modern times and provided an odd contrast to the severe penalties. In AD 595, John Jejunator, Patriarch of

◄ Hippolitus, a christian prelate, tied to the tail of a wild horse and dragged to his death

Constantinople, devised a code of laws on the subject of penance. From these beginnings, the Christian religion increased its interest in punishment; indeed, the Church produced its own list of offences which could be punished both on earth and in heaven.

It was logical that Rome, as the centre of Christianity, should be the pace-setter for the rest of Europe on the subject of punishment. In Rome, beheading was considered a most honourable death, and so Europe adopted this method of execution for high-ranking persons. It is possible that the Romans also introduced the *fossa,* or ducking stool, to Britain. Excommunication could be imposed on drunken priests or laymen. Whipping was another Roman penalty used mainly on schoolchildren and military offenders. They used slender rods; the *bastinado* was employed in the Eastern countries. Russia called her whip the *knout* and it comprised interwoven thongs and wires. So great was the shock and wounding it caused that death was the inevitable result.

In the fourth century, the Emperor Valens drowned eighty prelates near Nicodemia because he could not pacify them over some grievance. The Codes of Theodosius and Justinian confined capital punishment in AD 438 to murder, treason, adultery, forgery if committed by a slave, and stealing. Spain and Germany followed suit by making murder a capital offence, whilst in Britain and Gaul, criminals were still sacrificed to the gods.

Other forms of punishment were appearing in Britain. In AD 304, St Alban was burnt at the stake for alleged heresy and so became the first person in England to suffer in that manner. Five hundred years later, Edmund, King of East Anglia, was taken prisoner by the Danes; on 20th November 870, he was bound to a tree, scourged, shot with arrows, and finally

◀ *fig 7* The Russians, too, employed animals for punishment

beheaded because he refused to renounce his Christian faith. His torture occurred at Bury in Suffolk and he was subsequently canonised; the place is now Bury St Edmunds.

The fact that new or different penalties were introduced into England might be regarded as progress of a sort. At least it showed that some consideration was being given to the crime problem and further developments were to come. The Anglo-Saxons decided to punish murder merely with a fine. They executed only for theft; all other offenders, even killers and rapists, were fined or suffered one or other of the lesser penalties. Among these was the tumbrel-pond for drowning thieves, women in particular, or for ducking minor criminals. They had a *scealding* stool which might have been the forerunner of the ducking stool, and there remained the pillory, used in ancient Greece and Rome so many years before. The Anglo-Saxons called it the *healfang* or stretch-neck; the word *healfang* is very like the modern North Yorkshire dialect term for half-hang. *Scealding,* by the way, is similar to the North Yorkshire dialect for scolding, and scolding women in particular were ducked.

For a time, burning was inflicted for a small number of crimes involving property, based on the logic that a man's home and his crops were his sole wealth and livelihood. Following the early blood-for-blood thinking, if these were maliciously burned, it seemed sensible to inflict a like punishment on the culprit.

In the seventh century, Ethelbert I of Kent made what are probably the first English written laws. He listed fines for all offences and included a scale of compensation. Every part of a human body was given a value: Hibbert quotes that an eye was worth fifty shillings (£2.50 or $6.80 in today's values, though vastly more then); a foot carried the same value; a toenail was worth sixpence (2½p). Ethelbert did not agree with executions because they depleted his all-important fighting strength—every man played an essential part in defending the kingdom and no one could be spared. The fines he imposed were therefore severe and varied according to the rank of the victim and his assailant. A woman who committed theft, however, was drowned—she was considered dispensable.

When the Danes first arrived in England in the eighth century, they introduced harsh penalties, like throwing criminals from the tops of high cliffs (Fig. 8). They also introduced the *man-bot*, or the value of a slave. If a slave was killed, his killer had to pay the *man-bot* to the slave's master, as a form of compensation for the master's loss. Every man, from the highest to the lowest in the land, was given a value, or *wergild*. If a man was killed, his attacker had to pay *wergild* to members of the dead man's family. A woman had no value and neither had a criminal. The Laws of Wihtred said that if a thief was caught in the act, he could be killed without worrying about his *wergild*: in other words, his misdeeds rendered him worthless and his family received no compensation for his death.

After the death of Alfred the Great in AD 901, there developed a movement to replace fines with a system of physical violence. The public wanted revenge upon the criminal; it was felt that severe physical penalties would be a deterrent and therefore a safeguard. Whipping was considered such a penalty, and a thong of three cords knotted at the ends was used. When Ethelred II (978-1016) was a child, he was whipped by his mother. She didn't use a whip—she thrashed him with candles! It is said he feared them for the rest of his life.

In tenth-century Britain, mutilation also appeared on the scene. By this time, the method of execution depended upon the status of the criminal: a free woman was cast from a cliff or drowned; a male slave was stoned to death by sixty or seventy other slaves and if any of them failed three times to hit him, they were whipped—on top of that, every one who took part in the stoning had to pay threepence to the dead slave's master.

fig 8 Hurling from rocks

A female slave who stole was drowned. Later in the century, imprisonment was recommended for some crimes, but only if the suspect could not guarantee compensation to his victim. Hanging was employed and there existed laws against drunkenness and witchcraft, the latter carrying 120 days' imprisonment.

Canute's accession to the throne in 1016 introduced further new thinking to England. This famous king did not favour capital punishment, but said, 'We command that Christian men be not on any account for altogether too little condemned to death, but rather let gentle punishments be decreed for the benefit of the people.' His idea of gentle punishments was to cut off ears, noses, upper lips, pluck out eyes or scalp the evil-doer. There is little doubt this was considered gentle in his time. If, however, a rogue was willing to mend his ways, Canute was willing to help. He considered social problems, the causes of crime, and such problems as old age, poverty, youthful misdeeds, sickness and whether a culprit was a slave or a freeman. He also distinguished between wilful acts and unintentional ones or accidents. Canute died in 1035 after a reign blessed with peace and public security, and undoubtedly crime then increased again.

By 1039, the executioner once more held a high position in society. The Normans, who arrived in 1066, valued his services, but not necessarily to *kill* criminals: William the Conqueror preferred to mutilate them, and found the executioner the fellow for the job. William was crowned king on 25 December 1066 and began a new chapter in England's judicial advancement. One of his first royal speeches proclaimed that 'I forbid that any person be killed or hanged for any cause', and for nearly forty years afterwards no criminal was hanged in England; yet in the next breath the order was 'Let their eyes be torn out and their testicles cut off', and such injuries resulted in many deaths. There did exist alongside these mutilations many lesser penalties. There were countless tiny prisons in manor houses, castles and similar places. The Normans built prisons in castle dungeons, chiefly to lock away enemies rather than criminals.

Upon his arrival in England, William had found that lords of the manor and bishops were the main guardians of the peace; the bishop and an alderman, as joint judges, sat in the shiremoot. William decided to put the bishops in their own courts to deal only with ecclesiastical offences, leaving the shiremoot free to cope with crimes against the people. All clergymen were tried at the ecclesiastical courts, but laymen were tried there only if they committed ecclesiastical offences. Cunning laymen realised that the penalties in the bishops' courts were less harsh, so upon being charged with an offence, many persons claimed to be clergymen to win the benefit of an ecclesiastical trial. This became known as 'benefit of clergy'. It must be remembered that clergymen were among the few educated people, and it seemed even to the simplest peasant

fig 9 500 years later the Germans still practised tortures similar to those inflicted by Canute and William the Conqueror in eleventh-century Britain

that the educated man was dealt with more leniently than his fellows. It also began to seem as if there was one law for the rich and another for the poor—for instance, when the church imposed pilgrimage as a penance, a rich man would pay a 'professional pilgrim' to make the journey; or a fast of thirty-nine days could be completed in three days if a man could pay twelve others to assist him.

William's abolition of the death penalty did not survive. In fact, it was his own son who created the first subsequent capital offence. William Rufus was a passionate hunter who hunteu day and night and thought of little else; it was natural enough for him to order death for those caught hunting deer in the royal forests!

Henry I, another of the Conqueror's sons, followed Rufus to the throne. He inherited a problem of rising crime from Rufus' carefree days which was aggravated by the poverty of his subjects. They could not pay the fines which had been introduced by the Anglo-Saxons and were still invoked; compensation was also difficult to enforce. Prisons were comparatively few and in any case were meant to detain suspects rather than punish offenders. In Henry's mind there was only one solution: he extended capital punishment to embrace more than Rufus' solitary capital offence. Before such sentence could be inflicted, the courts had to be completely satisfied that a suspect was guilty and ingenious methods existed to determine this, based on the belief that only one Being could possibly know the accused's true state of mind— God alone could determine innocence or guilt; but to help him in these decisions, trials by water or fire were devised.

Ordeal by cold water involved casting the suspect into a pond. The water was blessed by a priest, the theory being that pure water would reject an impure person; the guilty would float and the innocent sink. All suspects were tied to a rope in case they had to be hauled out. For ordeal by fire, the suspect had to grip a red-hot iron bar while he walked nine paces.

Afterwards, his hand was bandaged and if, three days later, his skin was not scarred, he was considered innocent. There was also a combination of the two—ordeal by hot water. The hand was plunged into boiling water to grasp a stone. If it was free from scalds three days later, the suspect was innocent. Clergymen underwent the ordeal of coarsened bread. Priests swallowed bread containing feathers; if they choked, they were guilty.

By 1100, public penance was on the decrease in England, although it was practised on the continent. Even emperors were not exempt. Emperor Henry IV of Germany, who had been excommunicated by the pope, went to Rome in an endeavour to have his sentence removed. He was made to lie on the snow, clad only in the traditional penitent's white dress, as he awaited the pope's decision. For two days he lay there, fasting and frozen, an object of fun for the onlookers, until, on the third day, the pope relented and pardoned him.

In fact there appeared in 1103 what might have been the first true English prison. Thieves were incarcerated at Baulk House in the High Street, Winchester. This place of detention closed in 1115, a mere twelve years later, and it is uncertain whether it was a national prison (Winchester was then the centre of government) or merely a sheriff's prison for the county of Hampshire. At any rate, it may well have set a pattern for the future.

In addition to death and imprisonment, many minor penalties were enforced, like the age-old game of subjecting the offender to ridicule in the hope that others would be deterred. A baker who gave short weight in bread was paraded through the town with loaves around his neck. A fishmonger who sold bad fish was draped with his wares and dragged around the streets. This type of penalty was a relic of the Church's attitude to punishment, for degradation had long been considered suitable for those who sinned or committed minor offences.

fig 10 A baker drawn to the pillory with a short weight loaf tied to his neck

Henry I continued to introduce new capital offences. In 1124, forty-five suspects were charged at Leicester with crimes like murder, treason, burglary, arson, robbery and theft; all these carried the death penalty. Four years later, Rannulf Flambard died in the Tower of London, its first prisoner. This famous building was later used to detain all kinds of prisoner— political, military and criminal. The use of prison as a crime deterrent was gaining ground. In 1140, Brian Fitzcourt built a cell called 'Cloere Brien' at Wallingford Castle to accommodate William Martel; some authorities believe it was the first specially-built prison. The king made *public* gaols the responsibility of the sheriffs. This is still so in some English counties. One of London's most infamous public prisons already existed around this time; in 1155, the sheriffs of London and Middlesex claimed an allowance for repairs to Fleet Prison, even though it was only partially completed. Warders were used and there is record of the sheriff of Hampshire paying wages to the king's gaolers, though some sheriffs had their own gaols—the 'county gaols', which retained this name until 1878.

Like the Tower of London, they were used for all manner of offenders, even prisoners of war or hostages. Thieves, then known as *latrones,* were detained there.

In 1154, however, Henry II had come to the throne. He was destined to win fame as a reformer and was responsible, among other things, for the introduction of a centralised judicial system, with travelling judges who enforced the law in the king's name. Henry disliked 'benefit of clergy' and the ease by which persons could escape punishment. He realised that the English law needed sound reform. With courageous enthusiasm, he tackled the problem and within a dozen years had radically changed the situation. He set a personal example by publicly doing penance for the death of Thomas à Becket and ordered the construction of prisons in every county where none existed. He wanted them to be used to confine 'presumptive evil-doers', and as a result suspects were detained until they were either bailed or appeared before a court. This system still operates. Henry wanted his prisons to be sited in the boroughs and cities, and, if possible, within the castles. No other official guidance was given. If a castle was not available or suitable, new buildings had to be erected and the sheriff had to make sure the work was done.

Henry II laid down that the punishment for robbery, murder and false coining should be amputation of the right hand and right foot, instead of death. Trial by ordeal was still permitted to determine the guilt or innocence of thieves who stole objects of less than five shillings value, and anyone found guilty of that offence lost a foot.

Henry's spate of prison building left only five counties without a prison: two of them were palatine counties (Durham and Chester); the others were Herefordshire, Rutland (said to be too small) and Westmorland (said to be too remote and undeveloped).

As the thirteenth century approached, therefore, England was undergoing one of her many periods of legal reform. By

1182, Southampton possessed its first municipal prison. This was the first of its type in England and was financed from the profits of the borough farm! But unlike his legacy, Henry was not immortal. He died on 6 July 1189 and was followed to the throne by his son, Richard I.

3 Justice Must Be Seen
1200 - 1558

In 1210, King John summoned a council in London's Bridewell Palace—a building which later gave its name to the early English prisons—to discuss the royal finances. This century also witnessed the erection of the Marshalsea, another famous, or infamous, English prison. Detention began to meet with the approval of officialdom; though desire to reform the criminal was not the sole reason for the popularity of the prisons. Vast and illicit fortunes could be made by their owners or managers.

With this gradual change in penal methods came some new thinking on the whole question of trial and punishment. Around 1215 trials by ordeal became less frequent. This

fig 11 Prisoners in the sixteenth century detained in chains

may have owed something to the ideals expressed in Magna Carta, although Pope Innocent III had the final say in the matter. When the fourth Lateran Council met in November 1215, the pope instructed his clergy not to take part in trials by ordeal. All over Europe this caused problems of law enforcement. Hitherto, priests were considered indispensable, without the help of God's representatives on earth, there could be no satisfactory method of establishing a person's guilt or innocence. For a time, the judges tried to organise ordeals without the priests, but their efforts lacked the necessary authority and trials became meaningless. Chaos often resulted, with thousands of untried prisoners crowding the gaols. Because there was no method of trying them, they were set free. And then, as Bressler puts it, 'someone had the idea of using jurors of presentment'. Already in England these

fig 12 The stocks continued for centuries as a popular way of
degrading minor offenders.
Man and woman in stocks—'A stockes to staye sure and safely detayne
Lazy, lewd leuterers that lawes do offend' (Harman's 'Caveat', etc)

fig 13 Stocks and whipping post on a village green in Rutland

'jurors' *presented* the accused for trial and gave evidence against him, but now actual trial by jury had become a reality. The system and its workings were far from perfect in the early days, but at least it formed a basis for the system still found in countries all over the world. All manner of penalties were at the disposal of the early courts, but imprisonment was used to a large extent. In 1222, two blasphemers were sentenced by the Council of the Province of Canterbury (held at Oxford) and sent to a bishop's prison to live on bread and water. In the same year, an entire Lincolnshire jury was imprisoned for giving a false verdict, and soon afterwards, a man was imprisoned for holding lands to which he was not entitled. A sentence of imprisonment could occasionally be terminated by the payment of a suitable fine; consequently moneyed relatives or friends would come to the rescue and the gaolers made a little ready cash.

The ever-popular stocks were in use, too. A set at Wallingford was in reality a combination of stocks, whipping post and pillory; an account of 1231 records a repair to this formidable edifice, so it was probably in use long before this date. The stocks were not considered a hard penalty; they punished minor offenders for whom degradation was deemed suitable. Some early references to imprisonment really meant a spell in the stocks.

Outlawry was extensively practised. In 1221, the justices in eyre visited Gloucester to try some 330 acts of homicide. They decreed 1 mutilation, 14 hangings and over 100 orders for outlawry; we are not told what happened to the other suspects. The origin of outlawry lies deep in history. There are references in Anglo-Saxon times when an outlaw was known as a *frendlesman* because he lost all his friends. He was an 'outlaw against all the people' and the notion might have developed when people ran away from their forthcoming punishment or escaped from sanctuary. When a man was declared an outlaw, he lost the protection of the law; the import of the sentence is contained in the phrase *caput gerat lupinum*—let him be treated as the head of the wolf—which was the legal term used to declare him an outlaw. Thereafter, every man's hand was against him. Neither he nor his relatives had any redress; his house could be burned, his land ravaged and he had no hope of reprieve. It was a terrible sentence, particularly as it affected his family, too.

By the Norman era, the tiny hundred courts of England could inflict this penalty even against a defendant who failed to appear before them. It was the custom to call an accused at three successive courts, and sentence of outlawry was pronounced if he failed to answer the final call. By the thirteenth century, the number of calls had increased to five.

As he had legally ceased to exist, an outlaw could be killed by anyone at any time, anywhere. By the thirteenth century, this harsh rule was modified so that such killing was justified only if he defended himself or ran away. Even so, many authorities did feel his lot was too rough, and eventually the life of an outlaw was deemed to be in the king's hands: anyone who killed him without reason was liable to a charge of homicide.

An outlaw's lands and property passed into custody of the king, who held them for a year and a day, after which time they passed to the lord of the manor. The penalty offered tremendous temptation to unscrupulous justices and may have been one reason for the popularity of the sentence.

Henry III recognised the possibilities of acquiring land when in 1255 he outlawed over seventy murderers and obtained their property. Fines also helped him by swelling his funds. In 1256 Northumberland justices tried 77 suspected murderers; 72 were outlawed. In 1279 they heard 68 cases of murder, and 64 convicted killers were outlawed. Apart from the property angle, outlawry was an easy sentence to pass. It later became possible to end a sentence of outlawry by becoming 'in law'. If the outlaw placed himself before a jury for a new trial, he could become a 'new' person; but he had of course lost all his lands and goods and as a 'new' person was not entitled to their return. In later years an outlaw's land was recoverable, but never his chattels. This was not unique to England; the outlawry system was widespread in Europe.

In Italy at this time self-punishment was considered a problem. Flagellation developed into something of a national pastime, and people could be seen marching through the streets whipping themselves beyond reason, a practice that spread to Germany and France. It was checked when Pope Clement VII stepped in and outlawed the flagellants, and by earnest and official efforts on the part of the worried authorities this grotesque expression of religious guilt more or less disappeared, though it was found again in the fourteenth century and in Germany in the fifteenth. The practice seems to have been associated with natural disasters: the Black Death, for instance, killed over 25 million people in Europe, and a crop of newly created religious sects took the blame for it upon themselves, punishing themselves in anticipation of an imminent Day of Judgement.

In 1241, hanging, drawing and quartering occurred for the first time in England. The victim was drawn by horses to his place of execution. In early cases, he was hauled on his bare back across the cobbles, but this inflicted such serious or fatal injuries that a sledge was later introduced (Fig. 14). He was then hanged, sometimes until he was dead or, if he was unfortunate, until nearly dead. Finally he was quartered, ie he was disembowelled and his body cut into small pieces. The penalty should therefore read 'drawn, hanged and quartered', but few, if any, references describe it as such.

At about the same time, Henry III passed his famous statute *Assisa et panis et cervisiae*—the assize of bread and ale—to regulate the price of corn and to ensure that minor transgressions were not overlooked. This made it unlawful for

fig 14 The gunpowder conspirators in the seventeenth century

were drawn to their execution

bakers to break the laws of their trade; offenders could be placed in the pillory.

The public was growing more cunning in its dealing with the law. Convicted felons and their families forfeited all their goods. Accused persons reasoned that if they refused to plead, they could not be tried; without a plea, the trial could not continue. About 1272, the authorities under Edward I decided to force them to plead. Unwilling suspects were put in a 'strong and hard prison'. They were cast in irons and made to lie on the floor in the worst possible part of the prison, among rats and vermin. They were fed on a portion of stale bread one day and stale water the next. But this did not break the really stubborn and there developed the practice of heaping immense weights upon them in the hope it would compel them to say something. Many died under this pressure, but others succumbed and uttered their pleas. This torture became known as *peine forte et dure*—strong and hard pain—and was practised all over Europe (Fig. 15). It was not considered a punishment; it was a method of inducing a plea. One of England's newest saints, Margaret Clitherow of York, died by this method and was canonised in 1970. The pattern was similar elsewhere.

In 1300 a machine was used to behead five men at Zittau, in Germany. Hitherto, the axeman had been the traditional executioner, but fearsome and clumsy results often occurred. Was Germany's the first machine? There is a strong belief that Conrad of Swabia was despatched by the Italian *mannaia*, or 'herdsman's axe', at Naples as early as 1266, and in 1307 there was a similar device in Ireland. It was used 'near to Merton' to execute Murcod Ballagh and was probably the first *authentic* example, though Italy certainly had a very early beheading machine, and England had a well-used one in

◀ *fig 15* Peine forte et dure—William Spiggot under pressure at Newgate

Edward III's reign (1327-1377). This was the notorious Halifax Gibbett, the base of which can still be seen not far from Gibbett Street in Halifax, Yorkshire. This is not to be confused with the gibbets used for hanging dead bodies. Some authorities believe the Halifax Gibbett was brought to England by the Normans; certainly, guillotine-type machines existed long before Monsieur Joseph Ignace Guillotin was immortalised in France. The Halifax machine beheaded on market days—usually Tuesdays, Thursdays and Saturdays—and victims were executed on the first market day following conviction. Occasionally, a callous twist was introduced in the execution. If a man had stolen a horse, pig or sheep, the animal in question was hitched to a rope, which in turn was tied to the gibbett's blade. When the animal walked away, it drew the blade high within its frame, whereupon the rope was cut. Down came the axe. If no animal was involved, the blade was hauled up by the bailiff, who also cut the rope.

The use of animals to punish convicts at Halifax contrasted with other countries who punished erring beasts! In 1386, a French sow was dressed up as a woman and hanged for biting a child; in 1389, in Dijon, a horse was hanged for kicking a man. Judicial oddities did not end here; for example, French bankrupts had to wear green caps. In London, a John de Hackford, who had been spreading stories that ten thousand men were about to rise and slay the men in power, was sentenced to imprisonment for a year and a day, to stand in the pillory for three hours once every quarter without hood or girdle, unshod, and to have a whetstone hung by a chain from his neck marked with the words 'a false liar'; and 'there shall be a pair of trumpets trumpeting before him on his way'.

Perhaps it is well to recall that punishments were essentially a public affair in those times. Executions, in particular,

fig 16 An American pillory ▶

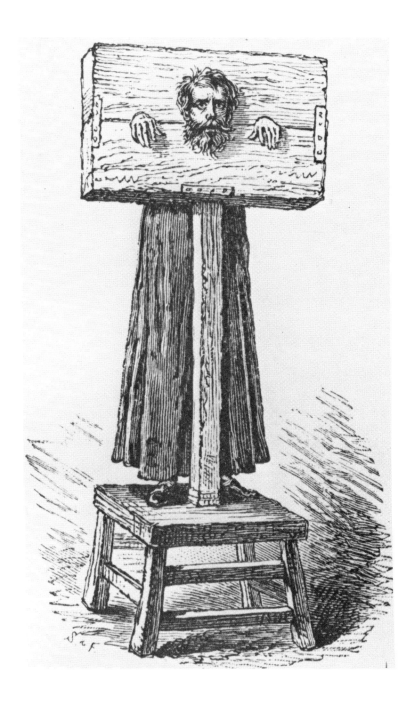

fig 17 The stocks provided entertainment for the public

were something of a social event and for this reason their exact method mattered a great deal. Drowning was a woman's penalty and degrading for a man; therefore, men were occasionally executed by this method. By far the most superior method was to have one's head cut off with a sword or even an axe, and this was reserved for noble men. Hanging, drawing and quartering was becoming more frequent in Europe.

Prison became a fashionable penalty, rather than a place of detention, and in 1373 the men of Southwark were licensed to build, in what is now Borough High Street, 'The Court of the Marshalsea of the Household and its prisoners'. Crime continued to increase—or to attract more attention—and only three years later members of the House of Commons actually knelt and prayed that every village in England be equipped with the stocks. By 1405, parliament realised that more positive measures had to be taken and passed an act to compel all villages to have stocks. A place without them was regarded as a hamlet and no self-respecting village wanted such a classification. Quite suddenly, stocks were fashionable. The lords of the manor even had their own movable stocks constructed to punish servants. Stocks were cheap and required little or no supervision; furthermore, they provided pleasant entertainment and exposed a villain to public scorn and sport.

A popular public spectacle was the cucking stool, used against petty female offenders. It was occasionally employed alongside, or instead of, the ducking stool. The ducking stool was used to duck scolding women; the cucking stool originally served a different purpose. Offenders were seated upon it and carried through the town to be laughed at. A decision by Leicester's local authority in 1467 is a good indication of its merits. It directed that scolds were to be punished by the mayor on a cuck stool 'before their own doors and then carried to the four gates of the town'. The cuck stool has been described as a 'seat of infamy, where strumpets and common scolds with bare feet and head, were condemned to abide the derision of those who passed by'. Other more lurid accounts suggest that far more womanly flesh was bared, for some cucking stools had a large hole in the seat! Scottish ale wives who sold bad ale

52

DUCKING STOOL, AS PRACTISED AT BROADWATER,
NEAR LEOMINSTER.

DUCKING-CHAIR AT A VILLAGE WELL.

fig 18 Ducking stools

were put on the cucking stool. As a matter of academic interest, the ancient common law offence of being a 'common scold' was only legally abolished in England with the Criminal Law Act of 1967! More seriously, prison building continued apace. Ludgate had opened in 1378 and by 1419 was a debtors' prison. Debtors did not always seek release by paying up when they could: prison provided a bed, food could be bought or brought in by relatives, and the gaol was regarded by those with money as a common lodging house where criminal plots could be hatched. But prison sentences were by now popular with the authorities and in the cities were tending to replace fines, or to be offered as an alternative. In London, for instance, wounding with a sword carried a penalty of either a £1 fine or forty days' imprisonment. In rural parts, however, prison was still a rarity. If a man was sentenced to imprisonment in an area with no local gaol, another man would be hired and handcuffed to him until a prison could be found.

In 1423, Sir Richard Whittington died and left money to re-build Newgate Prison. Gradually, the great prisons of England began to supplement the host of smaller ones and outside each one stood the traditional gallows. By the mid-fifteenth century, this was by far the most popular method of execution in England, in spite of highly tasteful and competitive foreign methods. Almost every man of note had his own gallows—one Italian nobleman even adorned his front door with a set which he repaired each year. In England, the right to hang felons was given to every town, abbey, castle and lord of the manor, each of whom owned at least one set of gallows. The mayor of Hull was unique among mayors in owning a gallows: in his official role he was also a chief officer of the admiralty, simply because he was technically admiral of the Humber. It suited all concerned if Hull's gallows could be used for admiralty offenders and His Worship was the ideal executioner, if only in name. The gallows at Hull were therefore established in the Humber, below high-water mark, so they

fig 19 The Halifax Gibbett

could be used for all civil and naval executions. A truly
touching compromise! Counterfeiters, too, were hanged here.
They were also executed at the Halifax Gibbett, and such was
the joint reputation of these places of execution that coiners
would pray, 'From Hell, Hull and Halifax, Good Lord deliver
us'. Hanging did not deter all coiners, however—a German
executioner, a Meister Friedrich, was himself hanged for
coining!

In 1429 a lynching occurred, when a widow was executed
by other women for murder. This is the first recorded instance
of an execution without trial by unauthorised persons, though
the term 'lynching' does not seem to have emerged for another
century at least, and even then its origins are hazy.

In 1453, the prisoners of Ludgate (which had closed in
1419, re-opened, closed again in 1431 and opened yet again)
were transferred to Newgate because they complained of
suffocation by smoke from a nearby fire. In 1463, Agnes
Forster, a fishmonger's wife, set about enlarging Ludgate. She
became just one—possibly the first—in a long line of unofficial

penal reformers. Without persons of her calibre to urge the authorities into action, many reforms would never have appeared. Reform of the penal system was to prove an uphill task.

Heresy has always been punished by burning. Whether it had something to do with hell-fire is uncertain, but religious offenders the world over have suffered this fate. In 1401, the burning of heretics was legalised in England, although earlier isolated cases had occurred. The Statute of Heresy empowered bishops to arrest all preachers of heresy, all schoolmasters who taught heresy and all owners and writers of heretical books. The bishops could gaol these people, whereupon the heretics in question were asked to abjure the realm, ie to promise to leave the country. If they refused, they could be burnt 'on a high place'. The first victim was William Sautre, a parish priest at Lynn. Although the law was repealed in 1533, Henry VIII saw fit to revive it in 1559 (Fig. 20).

As the end of the fifteenth century approached, the farce of pleading benefit of clergy was creating serious problems. The ecclesiastical courts punished a man spiritually. They could not inflict the death penalty, so any clergyman charged with a crime which carried death or imprisonment made sure he claimed his privilege, which had been so extended as to include even door-keepers and exorcists. Because priests were among the few literate people, the test of one's membership of holy orders was to read the first verse of the fifty-first psalm:

> Have mercy upon me, O God, according to thy loving kindness; According to the multitude of thy tender mercies, blot out my transgressions.

It became a simple matter for criminals to memorise the verse. The custom was to ask a convicted person if he had anything to say before sentence was passed and it was at this moment that he could put forward his plea of benefit of clergy. By repeating the Neck Verse, as it became known, he obtained what amounted to a reprieve.

fig 20 The burning of Edward Underhill fig 21 Painswick stocks—the modernised version

fig 22 Breaking on the wheel (France)

The ignorant felt it was a privilege enjoyed only by the educated and legislators began to create offences which were non-clergyable, ie which did not carry the right for anyone to plead benefit; for example, in 1496 an act stipulated that a person who killed his lord, master or sovereign could not plead benefit. Henry VII went further by saying that everyone convicted of a clergyable felony had to be branded on the thumb. This stopped persons claiming benefit on more than one occasion.

These actions indicated that some reasoning was going into the creation of laws; in 1477, Chief Justice Brian's words that 'the devil alone knoweth the thought of man' made due distinction between deliberate and accidental wrongs. In 1500, a very great man was made the laughing stock of his village—

a rare occurrence. Cardinal Wolsey came home drunk; for this, he was placed in the stocks by a justice called Amias Poulette! So there was to be some effort to make even the great obey even minor laws, although Poulette was a brave man to carry out the penalty.

When Henry VIII came to the throne, he soon learned he had judicial problems on the Welsh borders, where powerful lords enforced their own brand of justice. One of Henry's first successful campaigns was to overthrow them, and so began his reputation as a powerful ruler—which he consolidated by becoming the first and only English king to permit Sunday executions and boiling to death as a legal penalty.

Henry's hard line was firmly pursued. In 1512 murders in church or on the highway were classified as non-clergyable, suspects thus becoming liable to the death penalty, which Henry extended in 1536 to piracy, murder, rape, sacrilege, highway robbery, abduction, some burglaries and housebreaking. The whole of Europe was at this time experiencing a movement towards severity—and brutality—of sentence. In France, breaking on the wheel, properly done, had been acceptable although with no legal basis; it was now legally adopted, and spread to Germany.

In England, Henry's Whipping Act, introduced in 1530, was directed against the numerous layabouts who wandered the rural roads begging and stealing. His laws ordered them to be tied to the tail end of a cart, stripped naked and beaten through the town or village until their 'body be bloody by reason of such whipping'. The sentence was the same for men, women or children. Later, the act was amended to allow the victims to be stripped only to the waist, although Henry extended his campaign by ordering that anyone who gave alms to a beggar must forfeit ten times the amount he gave. Another of Henry's penalties was to cut off the ears of those who did not attend church; there was a special tool for this job. Banishment was also employed: in 1534, a woman was banished from Sandwich for immorality. If she returned, she was to be set upon the 'coqueen stool'—cucking stool.

During the 1530s, a new form of punishment began to manifest itself in France: a term in the galleys. In ancient times various nations probably used this as a punitive measure; the Corinthians' *triremes* were in use as early as BC 786. These were fitted with three rows of oars; the Byzantine empire had lighter galleys, with two sets of oars, known as *dromones,* and during the Middle Ages galleys with one bank of oars were used by the Venetians and the Genoese. The latter had introduced them to France during the reign of Charles VI (1380-1422). The French called them *bagnes* and although they had long been used to punish prisoners, they were not legalised for this purpose until 1532. In 1564 the length of time spent in a galley was restricted to a maximum of ten years. The end of enforced galley service did not come until 27 September 1748, when the office of captain of the galleys was abolished by Louis XV.

Back in England, Sir Thomas More was beginning to agitate for a more enlightened approach to the crime problem. He even suggested that reformation of prisoners was more beneficial than punishment. In Henry VIII's reign, a reputed 72,000 persons were executed in England, including the bold, reforming Sir Thomas himself. No one had listened to him, for it was a firm belief of the times that hard, tough punishment, not reformation, was the natural answer—indeed God's answer—to crime. Fines and prison were suitable for minor offences; death, or varying degrees of horror, must be the deterrent for the serious stuff.

Henry's sickly young son, who became Edward VI, opted for more compassion. Having repealed the laws permitting boiling alive, he also stipulated that poisoning was mere murder and not high treason. Yet he introduced mutilation for brawling or fighting in a church or churchyard, an action which won the approval of the church because it added excommunication to the temporal penalty.

In 1553 the ancient Bridewell Palace was given by Edward to the nation. He wanted it to be used as a home for the poor and impotent, installing a mill to grind corn; but by the seventeenth century the place had become a house of correction and 'bridewells' were born. (The original was destroyed by fire in 1666.) In 1576 every county in England was ordered to provide and maintain 'Abiding Houses, or Houses of Correction'. These bridewells were to be controlled by quarter sessions rather than by the sheriffs who had looked after the earlier prisons, and their aim was to provide food and work for beggars and those of similar misfortune. Eventually 300 of these institutions were in operation. Inmates were paid for their work, and on the whole were provided with good food,

fig 23 (a) Whipping at cart tail (b) A prisoner having his tongue bored while suffering on the pillory

clean linen and constructive discipline. Unfortunately as time went on the bridewells were absorbed into the general prison system, deteriorated and eventually disappeared. Had they survived, they might have proved ideal to cope with problem criminals. Instead, a viciously repressive treatment was continued.

Indeed, if anything this seemed to intensify. Even minor offences were savagely punished on occasion; not content, as of old, with fastening a man into the pillory, it became fashionable to nail his ears to the woodwork, or bore a hole through his tongue. As old records reveal, when the victim's specified time was over, 'he would rente his ears, one of the bedles would slit yt upwards with a penknyfe to loose yt'.

On 17 November 1558, Elizabeth I ascended the throne.

4 The Public Shows Concern
1558 - 1738

In general, Elizabeth was not noted for humanity towards her criminals. Estimated annual executions numbered around 800 at the beginning of her reign and increased steadily. One possible reason was that Henry VIII had not distinguished clearly between political and religious offences and Elizabeth executed many Roman Catholics for religious offences which, for legal purposes, were classified as treason—for instance the Jesuit saint, Edmund Campion, who was executed at Tyburn.

The English gallows was re-designed; during Elizabeth's reign, it became triangular-shaped. In Spain at the same time, execution by garrotting was favoured: the prisoner was placed in a chair with a high back, his head being fastened into an

fig 24 Gibbet irons and pillory (Note piece of skull in gibbet—said to belong to last murderer to be hanged in irons)

iron clasp with a screw at the back; as the screw was gradually tightened and he strangled, his neck was broken.

The Earl of Morton, regent of Scotland, was invited, in 1565, to witness an execution in England on the infamous gibbett at Halifax. He saw the huge, sharp iron blade suspended in a frame and watched it chop off heads. After seeing this beautiful piece of work, he went home full of ideas, from which he built a similar structure, the 'Maiden'. The name may have come from the Celtic *mod-dun,* meaning a place where justice was administered. Tradition says he was the Maiden's first victim; but although he did die on this very machine, his execution was not until 2 June 1581, some sixteen years after he built it. The first event was probably on 9 March 1566, when the assassins of Rizzlo at Holyrood Palace were executed. It is reported that the Earl of Argyll, when being prepared for execution by the Maiden, said, 'This is the sweetest maiden I have ever kissed'. Scotland in general followed English penal methods. At St Andrews in 1574, David Leyes was sentenced by a kirk session to appear before the congregation 'bairheddit and bairfuttit upon the penitent stool with a hammer in the ane hand and ane stane in the uther hand, as the twa instruments he mannisit his father'. His sentence was to stand for two hours in the jaggs and thereafter 'cartit through the haill toon'.

The jaggs were a device bolted into a wall and clamped around the prisoner's neck, holding him tight. They appear to be another name for the jougs, used occasionally in England and Holland. This was usually an ecclesiastical punishment; the jougs were often built into the exterior walls of churches, but there were many variations. In the north of England, it was the custom to nail the jougs to a church door or a tree in the church yard. Sometimes they were fastened to prison doors or even to the market cross. Churches up and down the country have preserved sets for modern inspection and it was

Sketched from the Life in Bethlem 7th June 1814 by G.Arnald Esq. A.R.A. Etch'd by G.Cruikshank from the original Drawing exhibited to the Select Committee of the House of Commons on Madhouses 1815.

WILLIAM NORRIS — AN INSANE AMERICAN

Rivetted alive in Iron, & for many years confined, in that state, by chains 12 inches long to an upright massive bar in a Cell in Bethlem.

this instrument that probably gave rise to the colloquialism 'in the jug', indicating imprisonment.

Scotland, in common with all European countries at this time, was experiencing the growing threat of witchcraft. This was as old as the hills, but in the Middle Ages a deep hatred, resentment and suspicion was felt for those who practised the magic arts. Unfortunate old people who were merely suspected of being witches were targets for abuse and derision by both the Catholics and Protestants. Furthermore, money could be made by catching witches, for witchcraft was considered a criminal offence in many countries: the Bishop of Geneva burned 500 suspects in three months, the Bishop of Wurzburg over 900; at one sitting, a senate at Savoy condemned over 800 to the flames. In common with European countries, England burned witches at the stake, a penalty which persisted a long time, the Bible being quoted as authority for it.

A more obviously dangerous pestilence in England was in fact indirectly working for reform inside the gaols. In 1577, the Black Assizes were held at Oxford Castle. This court earned its name from a plague known as gaol fever, a fearsome disease brought about by filth and grossly insanitary conditions inside the prisons. At this particular sitting it killed all present within forty hours, including the Lord Chief Baron, the sheriff and 300 other people. Obviously new ideas and a new authority were needed to cleanse the prisons, metaphorically and literally, but who was to do it? No one tackled the subject. At Exeter in 1586 another 500 died from raging gaol fever, and around this time a Mr George Savile of Halifax showed his concern over prison conditions by leaving £20 in his will for the building of a house of correction within seven miles of Halifax. It was built and survived sixty years, a small start on a huge task; over 300 years were to elapse before the prisons could be

◀ *fig 25* Iron harness similar to jaggs, used to confine the insane

fig 26 The scourging of Titus Oates from Newgate to Tyburn (from a Dutch print, 1685)

truly regarded as reformed—if that stage has ever been achieved.

Meanwhile, John Levytt was fined 4d for the petty crime of making a 'pair of shoes of unlawful stuffe' and several were fined for 'dogges unmuzzled'. Titus Oates suffered a rough ordeal after his false popish plot. He was pilloried, tied to a cart and flogged from Aldgate to Newgate; two days later, he was flogged from Newgate to Tyburn. The mob so roughly attacked him when next on the pillory that he was not fit to be flogged, but he recovered and was lashed into unconsciousness at the tail of a cart. Two days later he was lashed to a hurdle because he could not stand up, and flogged with hundreds of lashes— an eye-witness estimated them at 2,000, 'not even inflicted on a Jew or Turk or other heathen. It would have been merciful to hang him'.

Very individual penalties were occasionally meted out— a Jewish heretic was imprisoned and fed entirely on pork; a false witness had a red piece of cloth, shaped like a tongue, stitched to his clothes; drunks were made to walk around in cloaks made from barrels! (See overleaf). Devonshire Quarter Sessions ordered mothers and fathers of illegitimate children to be whipped.

In 1596 Elizabeth I extended banishment, her Vagrancy Act giving justices power to banish offenders to 'places across the sea'. Political offenders had been banished much earlier, but so far as criminals were concerned this was a new venture. It was one destined to reach massive proportions in the following centuries. On the face of it, removal of rogues from society was sensible enough, but no one troubled to think of the effects these men might have on the innocent recipients at the journey's end.

Banishment no doubt solved some problems, but the majority were still solved at the end of a hangman's rope. During the sixteenth century Tyburn in London became a notorious place of execution. It lay among trees at the corner

fig 27 The drunkard's cloak

of Edgware Road and Bayswater Road, near where Marble Arch now stands, and took its name from a small stream called the Tye Burn which ran nearby. (It is believed still to run underground to join the Thames not far from Buckingham Palace.) The site had been a traditional place of execution as early as the twelfth century, when the trees were utilised for hanging purposes. In fact the gallows became known as Tyburn Tree. The first execution here may have been that of William FitzOsbert, in 1196. He was a lawyer, known as Longbeard, who led an unsuccessful rebellion in London at that time. Victims were carried to Tyburn by cart from their cells in town, stopping at set places en route: the first was the Church of St Sepulchre, where the sexton tolled the bell and pleaded with the condemned to make his peace with Almighty God; prayers were said, the bell tolled again, and the procession moved off to the second stopping place, the Hospital of St Giles-in-the-fields, where a drink of ale was presented to the condemned person. When the hospital ceased to exist, the procession stopped at a local public house.

When Tyburn's sad trade became too brisk, a beam was erected right across Edgware Road to permit multiple executions (see p. 99). Stands were built to accommodate the public, who could witness events for a small fee, the cost being increased according to the rank or social standing of the victim.

As hanging became the acceptable British method of execution, drowning became less common, although it was occasionally practised in Scotland. A woman was drowned in Loch Spynie for theft and, as late as 1660, two more were drowned for denying that James VII of Scotland was entitled to rule the church according to his pleasure. Switzerland also drowned some of her criminals until 1652.

Another Scots penal method was the brank, used chiefly upon gossips. There were many varieties of this, but basically it was a metal clamp which locked around the woman's head

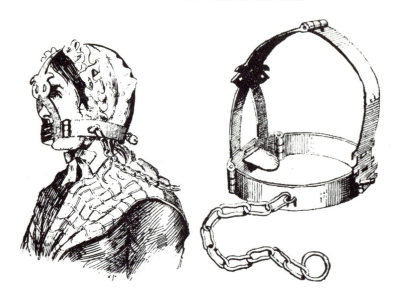

fig 28 Types of brank (Note the tongue-pieces)

and which bore a tongue-like protrusion (see p. 72). Sometimes this tongue had spikes on it; it was placed in the victim's mouth and she was then chained to a wall where the public could have sport with her. Instances occurred of husbands branking their nagging wives and leading them through the streets (see p. 74). The device was also used in England and on the European continent, and later a similar head-cage was used in American prisons, although not to silence noisy prisoners (see below). It may have been little more than a punitive adornment, worn to draw ridicule.

There was little change in the basic concept that punishment must either ridicule or destroy the criminal as the

fig 29 The American collar (1871)

fig 30 Husband and wife out walking

sixteenth century gave way to the seventeenth. The Japanese
dealt with adulterers by cutting off their heads and hacking
their bodies into little pieces, while Europe still burned witches.
In 1603, when James I came to the throne, England gained
a king who considered himself something of an expert on
witchcraft, on which he had written a work called *Daemon-
ology*, and he passed tough laws to counteract a threat which
he considered very real. It became a capital offence to 'enter-

tain, employ, feed or reward such a spirit, or any part of it, skin or bone', and the question of determining whether or not a person was a witch grew into a most serious affair. During James' reign, executions at Tyburn averaged about 140 a year and he tackled drunkenness with fines of five shillings (25p), or an alternative of six hours in the stocks.

It was in this century that gibbetts were first used, and these were not like the Halifax Gibbett. Ireland had already introduced the device for deterrent purposes. The notion was to suspend the bodies of executed criminals in chains near the site of their crime as a lesson to those who might copy their deeds (see p. 64). Occasionally, living criminals were

fig 31 The old dungeon at Bradford

hung in chains and left to die; sympathetic passers-by would shoot them to put them out of their misery. It is doubtful whether the gibbett deterred anyone.

As well as the ever-present crime problem, religious strife was again fermenting and in 1634, William Prynne, an MP, barrister and Puritan, was sentenced to life imprisonment for his faith. He was also fined £1,000, expelled from Lincoln's Inn, sentenced to have both ears cut off while in the pillory and branded with S.L., meaning seditious libeller. For a time, the Quakers found themselves bearing the brunt of England's oppressive penal system. Anne Aukland was imprisoned underground for some eight months in an open sewer with frogs and newts for company; at Colchester, James Parnell, another Quaker, was kept in a hole in a wall twelve feet above the ground. When George Fox was imprisoned in Scarborough Castle, he spent his own money to make his cell more homely, whereupon the warden moved him to another one which faced the North Sea and admitted rain and seaspray. Indeed, many of these squalid, damp dungeons were in old castles. Carlisle Castle, for example, had a dungeon containing a shelf a few feet from the floor where prisoners were manacled and chained by their necks. If they fell off, they hanged themselves. Even a well has been used as a prison. Another odd prison site was behind the local ale house, where the landlord was made responsible, though the majority of these little village rooms were mere lock-ups, places of detention rather than punishment. Similar dungeons were still to be found in halls and manor houses.

In England, soon after the accession of Charles I, Tyburn executions dropped to ninety per year. Not long after Charles repealed the laws on branding, he himself was executed. He was followed to the throne by his son, Charles II, who also took some interest in penal reform; a measure for which he was responsible was the introduction of the death penalty for anyone who killed another person during a duel. But Charles

fig 32 Building typical of a village lock-up. This type of construction was also used to cover wells, and it is often impossible today to know which was the building's original purpose

II died in 1685 without achieving much. In the same year, a bell was soundly thrashed for assisting heretics!

Virtually the only notable change in penal methods in this century was the gradual introduction of transportation. The first statute to use the word appeared as far back as 1662, and authorised the justices to transport such rogues, vagabonds and sturdy beggars as should be duly convicted and adjudged incorrigible to any of the English plantations across the seas. In 1666, this power had been increased when the judges were authorised to transport the moss-troopers of Cumberland and Northumberland to America for life, or, alternatively, to execute them. These freebooters had plundered the borders as early as 1272 and over the years, numerous stern measures had been directed against them.

With the transportation of criminals began one of the most infamous of Britain's criminal sanctions, though it did not become large-scale till around 1720 (see p. 81). Before it was fully under way, a man called Lynch was sent to America in 1687 on a mission to suppress piracy. He was given the power to dispense all acceptable penalties, but he added a few of his own. Some sources suggest that the term 'lynching' came from his activities, as he liked to execute criminals without trial. Other suggested origins indicate the term may have come from a Virginian farmer called Lynch who took the law into his own hands, or from a judge called Lynch who liked to hang people. Yet another suggested derivation is from James Lynch FitzStephen, mayor of Galway, who, in 1526, caused his own son to be hanged for murder in front of his own house (see also p. 54).

Another slight change in the savage penal climate, and a more enlightened one, was shown by the writ called the *breve de hoeretico comburendo,* which abolished the burning of heretics in England in 1676; although heresy, apostacy and sorcery were initially offences against the church, and church courts could not impose the ultimate penalty, such cases were

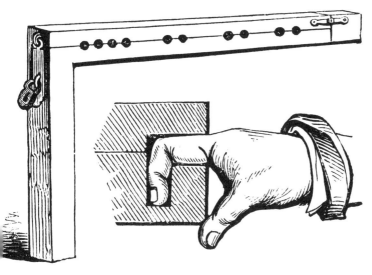

fig 33 The finger pillory

handed over to the criminal courts. The church did of course save many other offenders from death, particularly those guilty of more minor offences who managed to plead benefit of clergy. The last burning of a woman in Scotland was in 1708—and in 1710 the Maiden was finally put into retirement. Burning of witches continued in England for another eighty years or so.

By 1700 the death penalty was pronounced in England for high or petty treason, piracy, murder, arson, burglary, house-breaking, putting in fear, highway robbery, horse-stealing, stealing from a person to the value of one shilling (5p), and all robberies. This formidable list continued to grow—so that hangings, crudely and publicly performed, were frequent—and from this period any new statute would specifically state whether an offence was punishable without benefit of clergy. Five years later the system of requesting recital of the 'Neck Verse' was abolished, bringing to an end the farce of the benefit of clergy plea.

Butchery, cruelty and sadism remained an integral part of the penal system, even though some changes had come about. Punishment for minor transgressions reveals this most clearly. One unique example can still be seen in the parish church at Ashby-de-la-Zouche in Leicestershire: the finger pillory. The culprit's fingers were locked inside and bent at the knuckle, so that they could not be pulled free. He had to remain in that fashion for the specified duration of his punishment, and it was by all accounts a most painful experience for even a short time. Finger pillories were found in English schools to punish children, and in the great houses to punish servants.

In the early eighteenth century, England again had one of those periods of increasing crime, or increasing identification of it. Much concern was caused, for instance, by the appearance in 1712 of a group of youths known as the Mohocks. These were well-bred young men who terrorised the women of London by slitting their noses, wounding them and even putting them head first into barrels of tar and slashing their legs. All this for pure amusement—they held no malice against any particular woman, with the possible exception of some prostitutes. Men, too, were occasionally attacked. The spreading reputation of the Mohocks, plus the general increase in violence up and down the country—partly the result of political and social injustice and restlessness—led many citizens to arm themselves; the police could not cope, and real fear harassed the general public. House owners began to set mantraps or spring guns in their grounds; in 1713, Doncaster's authorities ordered that a whipping post be erected at Butter Cross. Violence in the street was resulting in retaliatory violence in the law and among the worried public.

Even so, when Queen Anne died in 1714, there were only thirty-two capital offences in England. Three years later, parliament authorised the beginning of regular transportation of criminals to America. Hitherto, they had been sold to planters

fig 34 The Botany Bay settlement

in the States or in the West Indies, and transportation had been spasmodic. Now it had fuller backing from the English judiciary and the system seemed an answer to prayer. It did sometimes work: some of the prisoners enjoyed the satisfaction of hard work in America's pleasing countryside, and even managed, upon release, to buy land or plantations in their newly adopted country, becoming successful farmers or businessmen. Those less fortunate perished in prison, or on the outward journey: conditions aboard the convict ships were atrocious enough to once more stir the lethargic public conscience.

Within England's shores, sectors of the public, by now more articulate and better informed, were indeed beginning to express concern about the severity of some sentences, and in particular about the ham-handed methods of carrying out certain penalties. Public opinion began to manifest itself and was growing into a force to be reckoned with.

On 3 November, 1726, Catherine Hayes was burned for the murder of her husband. This had long been deemed matter of course for women, but the executioners would show a tinge of sympathy for the victim of fire; they suspended her by the neck and strangled her before the flames did their worst. In Catherine's case, however, the fire was too hot and burnt the hands of the executioner. He released the rope and she fell into the fire in full consciousness, to suffer and die in acute agony. The public did not like this and let their feelings be known. On 19 January, 1728, Margaret Dickson was hanged for infanticide at Edinburgh. After being cut down, she was put in a coffin which was placed on a cart to be carried to Musselburgh for burial. The driver stopped at Pepper Hill for something to eat and Margaret sat up! She knocked off the coffin lid and climbed out; later she was proved totally innocent. Again the public made an outcry. In the same year, York Castle's treatment of its prisoners created concern. Many had died through permanently wearing leg or arm irons (see p. 83), which caused mortification. When the authorities finally had the humanity to appoint a doctor to treat the prisoners, some had been in irons for an unknown time—these consisting of a heavy collar for the neck, a large ring for the waist and two small ones for the ankles, all linked with a strong, heavy chain. In addition, many sets assembled with small men in mind were also used on large men.

It is appalling to learn that prisoners were charged a fee for the loan of their irons! Newgate, for example, charged three guineas for admission to prison, a further guinea for light irons, and half a guinea per week for a bed, with further fees for candles, knives, forks and fuel. It was of financial benefit to put as many irons as possible upon the miserable prisoner; logically, it was also a business venture to purchase a prison. If a man could not pay his fees, he was kept inside until he did,

fig 35 Man in irons

or until someone else paid for him. The longer he stayed, the more he had to pay. A good illustration of the farcical state of affairs within the prisons is shown by the case of John Bernardi, a political prisoner who died in Newgate in 1736. He had been inside since 1690—nearly fifty years—all the time without trial. He married in prison and his wife remained inside with him; he fathered ten children, all born within the prison walls. For the poor, then, there was little hope; a rich prisoner might enjoy his detention. Inevitably prison conditions could only deteriorate, when all that mattered was to make money for the governors, while tens of thousands of people, inmates and otherwise, died from that rampant gaol fever so feared for so many years. (In 1750 an outbreak at the Old Bailey killed fifty people, including the Lord Mayor of London.) The bungling, apathy and inefficiency displayed throughout the workings of the penal system continued as crime increased; perhaps it even fostered crime. The warders of both the Fleet and the Marshalsea prisons in London were arrested in 1728; each had paid for the privilege of holding the job, and now each was charged with murder and with robbery with violence. Prisoners in their charge had been manacled, tortured, confined in horrible corners, even starved or stoned to death. But in spite of this particular scandal, a further century and a half was to pass before things were radically corrected! In the early eighteenth century a man would pay as much as £5,000 for the privilege of being warder at Fleet Prison; he could sell it for the same amount and take a massive profit in the meantime.

The sad thing was that many prisoners were merely awaiting trial. They had not been proven guilty of any offence and yet were charged a fee for the use of the prison and its facilities. Even if they were proved innocent by the courts, they were promptly returned to gaol if they could not pay the outstanding warders' fees.

Major reforms had to come, if only in the efficiency with which brutal sentences were carried out. Particular public

fig 36 Irons used by Dick Turpin

fig 37 Sport at a multiple pillory

indignation seemed to be aroused by hangmen unskilled at their trade; throughout Europe a good hangman was admired, and few were available. Some swifter, surer means of execution was sought in many countries. It so happened that in May, 1738, a pregnant lady taking a walk in Paris happened to stroll past a criminal being put to death on the wheel, and was so upset that she was taken ill and the following day prematurely gave birth to a son. She christened him Joseph Ignace; the lady was the wife of a lawyer and her name was Madame Guillotin.

5 Reform in the Air
1738 - 1840

The baby Joseph Ignace Guillotin entered a Europe patently troubled by its crime rate, but with no idea of how to prevent crime and no understanding of any of its causes. A few years after his birth, however, in 1764, a young Italian, Beccaria, wrote his anonymous *Essay on Crime and Punishments,* a book which condemned capital punishment and repudiated the deterrent value of severe measures. He argued that public murder should not be used to prevent private murder, that life imprisonment was a better deterrent than death. An anonymous translation of the book appeared in England in 1767. Beccaria's views were far-sighted even by today's standards; whether they sparked off any particular

fig 38 Examples of prisoners' irons

reform is not known, but they must have fanned flames at that period beginning to kindle.

A case in 1748 typifies the confused yet troubled thinking of those times. William York, aged ten, was tried at Bury Assizes for stabbing a little girl; after the murder, he had buried the body. There arose a fierce argument about his criminal state of mind. Could a child of that age form a criminal intention? Did he know what he was doing? If so, did he realise it was wrong? Little William was found guilty and sentenced to death. On passing sentence, the judge said the law must take its course to deter other children from committing similar crimes. The home secretary did not agree with the judge's legal logic; he intervened and reprieved young William, but kept him in prison for nine years. He was pardoned at the age of nineteen years on condition he joined the navy. The home secretary's action suggests that other high officials were having second thoughts on the deterrent value of capital punishment. Questions were being asked as to whether this, or other savage penalties, did really prevent crime.

They were not easy questions to answer. English judges felt they did, and they administered the law. But legislators and others steadily sought improvements. The Society for the Promotion of Christian Knowledge and other would-be reformers had, for instance, joined the battle to convince authorities that change in the prisons must come. Many attempts fell on stony ground, but not all. The SPCK's efforts had borne fruit when, in 1729, a committee under the chairmanship of General James Oglethorpe was appointed to enquire into the state of the prisons in England. The general's discoveries shocked him; his committee were suitably appalled when told of prisoners fighting with rats for scraps of food. They heard of a man who took his dog into prison to protect him against vermin; it was killed by the rats. There was no water, no beds, no warmth. Sewers ran through some cells and others were steeped in what was politely called 'indescribable nastiness'. The committee warmed to its task and made a good job of it; it reported fairly and factually on all that it found. But no one did anything about it. No one in authority took action; perhaps no one had enough authority.

In 1755 John Howard began to agitate for prison reform, and he was not one easily fobbed off by official disinterest. He had served as a prisoner-of-war at Brest and knew something of prison conditions first hand. His work on the prisons became his life's quest, and he horrified hitherto apathetic politicians

fig 39 A perspective view of the execution of Lord Ferrers at ▶
Tyburn 5 May, 1760 for the murder of his steward

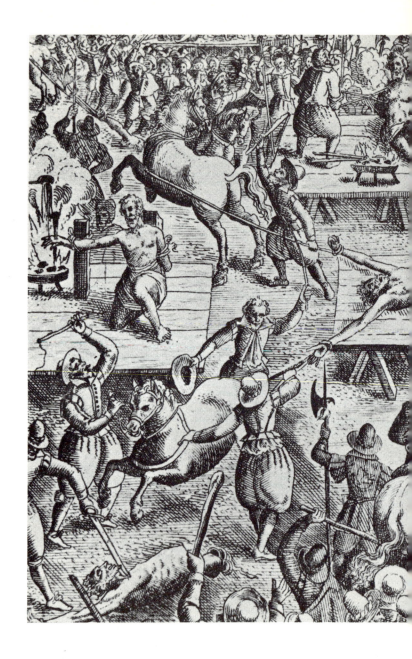

fig 40 The type of death suffered by Damien (The illustration shows

the death of Francois Ravaillac, who assassinated Henry IV of France)

with details of conditions inside. For example, his careful researches showed that convicts were placed in irons the moment they entered prison. This made them inactive from the start, and they remained so for the duration of their sentence. To John Howard, this seemed so pointless; the men could be given work to pass the time and to provide an interest; they could also serve their countrymen. The bishop's prison at Ely furnished further evidence for Howard. Men were chained to the floor on their backs, lying across iron bars. Others wore spiked collars around their necks, and iron bars crushed the legs of some; the filth was indescribable. By using such examples and a lot of persuasion, John Howard had managed, by 1774, to persuade the government to set up another committee to investigate prison conditions. Once again, all the committee's suggestions were ignored. Even when new legislation did reach the statute book, it did not always work as required: in 1774 parliament passed an act to abolish gaolers' fees, but the courts would not follow the spirit of the law. If a man could not pay the court's dues, he was simply sent to prison where he had no opportunity to earn money to pay his debt; the courts could not see the sense in releasing him.

An aspect that increasingly troubled the reformers was that throughout Europe the number of capital offences continued to grow, and executions were still made a public spectacle. Young people would form a large proportion of the crowd at any execution, and matured in a world that accepted brutality. The greater the standing of the victim, the more impressive the occasion would be and the larger the crowd. In 1760 a high gathering came to see the end of the Earl Ferrers in London—his request for a private execution had been refused. At nine o'clock in the morning the earl arrived at Tyburn in his private landau drawn by six horses; he was exquisitely dressed in white satin, embroidered with silver. Apart from the social cachet of the occasion, a new method of hanging was to be tried out. Hitherto, the hanged man had been left to choke by his own weight; for Earl Ferrers, the new 'drop' method was to be employed. Instead of strangling him, the rope, operated in conjunction with a dropping mechanism, would break the earl's neck to bring his life to a swift end. But the drop mechanism failed to work and Earl Ferrers, like thousands before him, choked to death. He was put in a coffin lined with white satin.

It was at this late period in history, just three years before Ferrers' death, that France inflicted what must be the cruelest death on record. Robert Francois Damiens had stabbed Louis XV and was tried for attempted murder. He suffered two months of torture and emerged for his execution on 28 May, 1757. Damiens, it is said, possessed phenomenal physical strength and on the morning of his execution, he was stretched on the rack and tortured. In the afternoon, the miserable man was taken to the Place de Creve where a crowd had gathered. Wealthy ladies carried smelling salts in preparation for their part in the ordeal, and as Damiens mounted the platform for his execution, he expressed a wish that he should be put quickly to death. This was denied. An eye-witness, the Duke of Croy, tells how six executioners bound Damiens to the boards with iron rings and began an afternoon of further inflictions. Finally a horse was harnessed to each leg and arm. The horses were whipped forward, intending to tear apart Damien's body. After an hour, they had failed even to sever an arm. When six more horses failed, the executioners cut his joints to make the work easier. Damiens watched them; he made no sound, but turned his head to kiss a crucifix. Two priests pleaded with him to confess as the horses tried again, and after an hour and a half, his left leg came off, quickly followed by the right. The crowd cheered; the right arm was pulled away and the remains of this sorry man were dragged to the ground. His hair had turned pure white and was shaved off. The limbs were collected and as two priests approached the remains, the executioners drove them off, saying Damiens was dead. But, according to

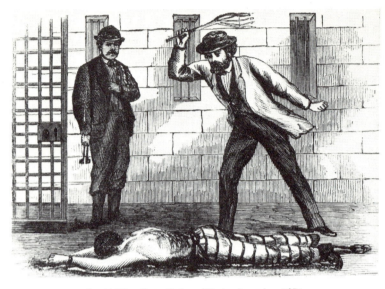

fig 41 The Cat—Prison life in America 1871

the Duke of Croy, this was not so! The trunk moved; the jaws
tried to speak and the eyes turned to the crowd, and finally,
Damiens died. He had not received the last sacrament and his
remains were burned, then scattered around. As the Duke of
Croy too truly wrote, 'Damiens suffered the greatest torment
that ever a man suffered in Paris, before my eyes and those of
many thousands of people, including many noble and beautiful
women.'

Whilst England's recorded horrors do not include anything to rival this, there were still plenty of vicious penalties.
When George II came to the throne in 1743, the courts considered pain and suffering to be the ultimate deterrent. Brutal
old punishments persisted: flogging was practised in the army,
where a new instrument, the cat-o-nine-tails, replaced the
earlier switches; whipping was common, too, among the
civilians, and in 1776, a writer called Cole tells of a ducking

stool in the Old Town Hall at Cambridge 'but made no enquiries about it'. In the same year, a magistrate commented that it was 'scarcely to be credited that by the laws of England, there are above 160 different offences which subject the guilty parties to the death penalty'. This number was to increase, but as transportation was increasingly substituted for it, America became flooded with British convicts; the legitimate settlers, who had their own social problems, including the treatment of offenders, to deal with, were beginning to question why they should tolerate the unwelcome visitors who were thrust upon them. They looked for a sound reason to end this unsavoury traffic.

This appeared in 1775 when war broke out, followed in 1776 with the American Declaration of Independence. No longer was America obliged to accept English prisoners, and she promptly refused. In England, this created an immediate problem—what could be done with all those hundreds of unwanted prisoners? Committees had reported very bad conditions within the gaols. Overcrowding was already a major problem and the magistrates refused to enlarge the buildings. There seemed to be no answer until the authorities remembered several old disused warships anchored in the Thames. It was decided to use them to accommodate prisoners, but only temporarily, until a suitable destination for renewed transportation could be found. Two ships were acquired, and later others in the Thames, the Medway and Portsmouth Harbour were added. This 'temporary' measure was destined to last for eighty years, and developed into terrible and oppressive cruelty, with men and boys chained in irons aboard the foul 'hulks'. One of the hulks was said to contain, at one time, one child aged 2, two aged 12, four aged 14 and twenty others less than 16 years old. Some were too young to dress themselves. As it was considered wrong to mix offenders guilty of different types of crime, an act of 1779 said that the hulks were to be used only for the 'more severe and effectual punishment for

fig 42 Hulks in the Thames

atrocious and daring offenders'. The prisoners were made to
work at dredging silt, sand and stone from the river, or to
help in the docks under firm supervision.

But as one door closed, so another opened. The world
conveniently provided another dumping ground for Britain's
unwanted scoundrels. In April 1770, Captain James Cook had
landed in Australia, at a place near Botany Bay. On 13 May,
1787, the first consignment of transported criminals was
despatched (Fig. 43). Eleven ships sailed to New South Wales
carrying between them a total of 558 male and 218 female
prisoners. The whole merry-go-round started again; more and
more prisoners were destined for transportation until the out-
going ships could not cope. The hulks accommodated the wait-
ing convicts until they were due to sail, but the rate of transportation was far too slow (see above). The hulks became
dangerously overcrowded, though this problem was alleviated
to a degree by allowing selected convicts to work ashore. The
women performed the domestic chores on board ship.

All this provided fuel for John Howard's agitation. He

had visited France, Switzerland and the Low Countries to examine prison buildings and penal methods; he also visited Germany. In 1777 he had published a book called *The State of the Prisons in England and Wales.* The result was the abortive Penitentiary Houses Act, 1779, which introduced the idea of a government-administered prison geared towards reform rather than punishment; it is possible, of course, that the abrupt cessation of transportation to America had forced the passing of this act. By this time, another reformer was making his presence felt. Henry Fielding, calling British prisons 'prototypes of hell', went on to suggest they were the most expensive places to live, and that they provided first-rate schools for crime. He

fig 43 Black-eyed Sue and Sweet Poll of Plymouth taking leave of their lovers who are going to Botany Bay

pointed out, that prisons were meeting places for prostitutes, drunks, forgers and coining syndicates, and a host of other felons. Between them, Howard and Fielding managed to create a wide interest in penal reform, but officialdom was still not convinced and the number of capital offences continued to increase. In 1714, there had been only 32 in England. Just over fifty years later, by 1769, there were 160; by 1819, the number was to rise to over 220. Official concern at the numbers of death sentences was, however, finally shown by the government, coupled with the possibility that the courts could make a mistake. Innocent persons might be hanged. Accordingly, a cabinet of between fifteen and twenty members was established, chaired by King George III himself. This gathering was to approve every capital sentence, except those for murder, before the execution was carried out. It became known as the Hanging Cabinet, but its work barely reduced the number of executions in England.

The persistent John Howard now produced some interesting facts about the wastage of life in prison, showing that some 4,375 persons were imprisoned, nearly half of them debtors; real criminals, in the main, were punished by transportation, pillories, whipping, hanging or burning on the hand. He concluded that most prisoners were: (a) debtors; (b) persons awaiting trial for felony; (c) persons awaiting trial, or serving terms of imprisonment, for misdemeanours; (d) those who failed to find sureties. In other words, very few had been convicted of serious crime. An earlier report claimed that over 5,000 persons died annually in prison through lack of food, but, although Howard's figures were impressive, it was to be a long time before any positive action resulted.

It was about this time—the 1780s—that the Gordon riots broke out in England. These were anti-popery riots named after Lord George Gordon, and the rioters' rampage escalated until portable gallows were carried around to hang them on the spot. A Bow Street runner reported seeing, on two occasions,

fig 44 A multiple execution in London

forty men hanged in a single day. Murders had become so frequent that a special act was passed whereby criminals were to be executed one day after being sentenced. The act went on to say that the body should be handed to the surgeons for dissection. Such was the incidence of hanging in London that it became known as the City of the Gallows. Violence had again come to the streets; in spite of Howard's efforts, it was met with increasingly stern judicial violence.

Others were taking up Howard's clarion: in 1771, a young barrister, William Eden, had called for the death penalty to be used only as a last 'melancholy recourse', but he was shouted down. The deep-rooted feeling that the dangers from violent crooks could only be met with legal severity reasserted itself, and, not content with hanging criminals, the authorities gibbetted their bodies on the roadside as a visible deterrent to others. Occasionally, a live victim was dangled in chains from the gibbett: in his book *Old Time Punishment*, William Andrews gives an instance of a highwayman called John

Whitfield who was gibbetted near Carlisle, and remained alive for several days until a passing horseman shot him to put him out of his misery. A man called Tom Otter was gibbetted in Lincolnshire for killing his bride of only a day, and, the story goes, a bird built a nest in his mouth.

The increasingly tough punishment being meted out in England had its counterparts on the continent. France still used burning, whipping, the wheel, hanging and branding, although Austria and Iceland had abandoned judicial drowning. It was in 1785 that Joseph Ignace Guillotin began to contemplate a device which would drop from a height and chop off a man's head. The idea was not original, but no one seems to have introduced the notion to the French before M. Guillotin. On 9 October, 1789, the year of England's last burning, the French assembly met to discuss a new penal code. M. Guillotin attended that meeting, seizing the opportunity to air his views, and suggesting that the French death penalty be decapitation. There should be no more torture; death should be instantaneous. Guillotin's suggestions brought Robespierre to tears, for he hated the whole concept of man deliberately destroying another man. Guillotin, not to be outdone, went on to suggest one penalty for all ranks; there ought to be no class distinction in judicial death. But the debate ended without a decision being reached.

England's proposed reforms smouldered on and a prison was built at Gloucester. Burning was *legally* abolished and a new voice joined those who cried for reform. Samuel Romilly, like Beccaria, wrote an anonymous treatise to air his views. Romilly had an advantage in that he was an accepted expert on the criminal law in his own country and on the European continent. Even so, his work had only a minor impact, but men like Howard and Romilly were doggedly determined. Howard, unfortunately, caught camp fever while visiting a sick woman in South Russia and died in 1790. But his work was to have a lasting effect. In 1791, the *public* whipping of women and girls

fig 45 The Paris guillotine

in England was stopped and the last man was gibbetted.

In France, prisons were overcrowded with murderers, and hanging continued in spite of Guillotin's marvellous idea. The assembly of France met to discuss the crime problem on 3 June, 1791. Total abolition of the death penalty was in fact suggested, but in the end, death by decapitation was approved. As Guillotin had wanted, there was to be no distinction as to the rank of the criminal, and on 20 March, 1792, a decree was issued to the effect that judicial decapitation would be carried out by mechanical means. This method was far superior to those of the other countries—Germany still used the sword for females, while Denmark used an axe for the lower social classes and the sabre for the elite. England had ceased to use the decapitating machine at Halifax, which left France in something of a unique position.

Three corpses were used to test the French device and the witnesses were astonished at the 'force and celerity' of its actions. Further tests on the corpses of women and children were satisfactory, though the device then failed on a male corpse. This setback was overcome by redesigning the blade, which, over the years, took various shapes. A doctor, Antoine Louis, favoured the convex shape; others preferred concave blades, whilst some liked wide sword-like shapes. The slanting blade eventually proved to be the most satisfactory. This was designed by no less a person than Louis XVI, and he died by that very blade. Apparently, no particular style was imposed by law, every manufacturer choosing his own.

In honour of its champion the device became known as the guillotine, and when the testing was over, the first genuine machine was built by Tobias Schmidt, a German piano-maker. On Tuesday, 15 April, 1792, it was tested on a sheep and later on five corpses; it had a slanting blade as Louis XVI had suggested, and performed perfectly. Soon the occasion of its first execution arrived. At 3.30 p.m. on 25 April, 1792, the Executioner of Criminal Sentences, Charles-Henri Sanson, stood at the side of his brand-new machine. It was thoughtfully painted red and the victim, Nicholas-Jacques Pelletier, was clad in a red shirt. His crime was theft and his death had been delayed to allow him to be the guillotine's first victim.

It was a triumph. France had seen nothing like it. In no time at all, a fanatical devotion arose in honour of the machine. Multi-bladers became the rage—a man called Guillot even experimented with a nine-blader at Bicetre. Some were built of metal, on wheels, for greater mobility, and a later refinement placed them flat on the ground. This meant the prisoner did not have to climb steps to reach the blade. The colour was changed from red to brown, and the blade shielded from view. Rubber shock absorbers were added because the heavy dropping blade made a horrible clanging sound as it rebounded after achieving its purpose.

Within a couple of years, the guillotine became France's new toy. It was nicknamed the People's Avenger, the Patriotic Shortener, the National Razor, Lady Guillotine or Saint Guillotine. It was originally called Louison or Louisette after the famous blade designer, but the name of guillotine stuck after it became the subject of a popular song. Victims actually paid to be executed by guillotine and children were given toy replicas to chop off birds' heads. Models were placed on the dinner tables of France, or made to contain perfume. In the latter case, the perfume container was in the shape of a doll whose head was severed to release the liquid. If this seems a ghoulish pastime, it is worthy of comparison with a toy introduced in America in 1971: a woman and a set of tortures to be inflicted upon her. She had a permanent expression of pain on her face and extra tortures were obtainable. Robespierre is said to have draped a guillotine in blue velvet for use at a religious ceremony.

But even the remarkable achievements of this brilliantly devised machine were not free from suspicion; some witnesses began to wonder if it killed immediately. There were suggestions that the victims' heads responded after severance— Charlotte Corday's face was slapped and showed annoyance. Medical tests were requested, but it is doubtful if a final decision was reached. Nor did the guillotine meet the whole-hearted approval of other countries. It remained essentially a French method of execution—hanging was favoured elsewhere.

As the nineteenth century approached, there began to appear some instances of moderation in the more absurd penalties in England. For example, 1799 saw the last use of the brank, on a blind beggar called James Brodie who was executed in July for murdering his boy-guide in Nottingham Forest; during his imprisonment before execution, Brodie was so noisy that the brank was used to silence him. And the pillory remained in use, too, to attract and entertain the crowds, contemporary writings giving highly picturesque accounts of the

actions of the fun-seeking mob. On 28 January, 1804, Thomas
Scott was pilloried at Charing Cross and pelted with rotten
eggs, filth, dirt from the streets, dead cats and rats. Another
victim was hooted at and suffered 'a torrent of popular
vengeance, blood, garbage, ordure from the slaughter house,
diversified with dead cats, turnips, potatoes, addled eggs and

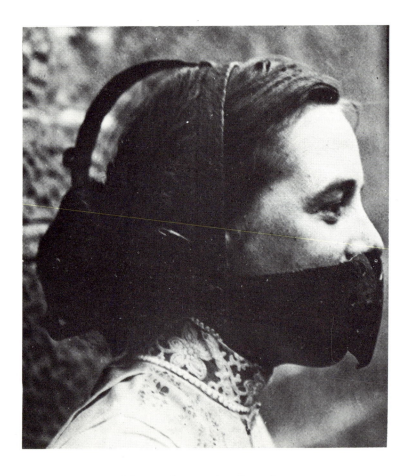

fig 46 The scold's bridle was also occasionally used on men

other missiles'. The sport was thought jolly enough, if only for the spectators. Behind such scenes, reformers were more concerned with the vast number of offences that still carried the death penalty. In 1799 London averaged an execution every fortnight. 1806 saw the start of the building of Dartmoor Prison which was to be used for prisoners of war. It became a convict prison in 1850 and during its construction, another famous prison reformer was at work. Elizabeth Fry was a specialist in women's prisons, and, in spite of her own eleven children, undertook a hard campaign to improve conditions. Samuel Romilly was also hard at work trying to rationalise and moderate criminal punishments by introducing amending bills in parliament. Many of his ideas were sound—in 1810, he introduced three bills to reduce the number of capital offences and followed this with a hard-hitting speech in which he tried to prove that certainty of punishment was a better deterrent than harshness. But his arguments failed to impress the government. He was not successful in his efforts to repeal three laws which carried the death penalty for minor offences such as stealing to the value of five shillings, or stealing to the value of £2 from houses or from ships in navigable waters.

Like the reformers before him, Romilly refused to be beaten. He later tried to introduce three more bills, then a further two, and enjoyed partial success when parliament abolished the death sentence for stealing from bleaching-grounds. The late John Howard's work was now bearing fruit, for an effort was made to classify prisoners. Their mental condition was beginning to be considered, and it was this type of small, significant change that encouraged Romilly to intensify the campaign.

In 1812 he won the repeal of the death penalty for sailors or soldiers who begged without a permit, though in 1817 he suffered a setback when the death penalty was reintroduced for men who damaged machinery. His struggle to have the death penalty lifted from shoplifters was a long and fruitless one:

in 1811, 1813, 1816 and 1818 he was rejected. His disappointment was acute, and when his beloved wife died Romilly killed himself, in a fit of despair. In 1819 there were still over 220 capital offences on Britain's statute book, embracing all manner of crimes and wrongs—including damaging Waterloo Bridge, or the impersonation of a Chelsea Pensioner!

Yet on the whole Romilly's theories and ideals were gaining ground. With the efforts of Howard, Fielding and Elizabeth Fry, he had helped create the urge to understand more about the criminal and about law and punishment. Though barbaric penalties were still enforced—in 1820 five conspirators were hanged and beheaded by a masked executioner, in 1827 a man called Moses Snook was awarded ten years' transportation for stealing a plank of wood and Mr Justice Park sentenced a man to death for stealing 2s 6d ($12\frac{1}{2}$p)—they increasingly tended to anger the bystanders. Romilly would have been delighted that the army had to be called in to quell the angry crowd when a body was beheaded and hanged—an action witnessed by the poet Shelley—in 1817.

Parliament took advantage of the upsurge in public interest to begin a massive law reform and in this were guided by yet another far-sighted reformer, Robert Peel. His formation of an organised police force had delighted the government, who chose him to guide parliament through the legal reforms; with his help, some 300 acts of parliament were expertly reduced to four new ones, thus ending capital punishment for numerous offences. It continued to exist for several, such as stealing goods worth over £2 in a dwelling house, but a massive change had arrived with little more than a stroke of the pen.

In keeping with public opinion, some juries did not favour capital punishment for the theft of trivial amounts; they would deliberately undervalue stolen property: one jury valued a £10 note at 39s (£1.95) in order to save the criminal from death; sheep stealing carried death, but another jury found a man guilty of stealing only the sheep-skin—no mention was made of

fig 47 Compulsory bath on board the convict ship HMS 'Success'.
Prisoners were pushed into the tank, the grating was closed and a
warder scrubbed them with a long broom

its contents; a horse thief was similarly found guilty of stealing horse hair! Branding remained a legal penalty, but now it was done symbolically with a cold iron on a piece of ham held in the convict's hands! Such leanings towards reform were encouraged in 1820 with the first hint of today's probation system: Warwickshire Quarter Sessions were passing one-day sentences of imprisonment on some youthful offenders. They were imposed on condition the youths returned to their parents or masters 'to be carefully watched and supervised in the future'. This bold step was unrecognised in law and was consequently studied with deep interest as a test of whether leniency could be effectively substituted for the harsher sentences.

New activities were being introduced into the English gaols, with the intention of giving the inmates something to occupy their minds or bodies. The treadmill (Fig. 48) was introduced by William Cubitt in the hope that some practical use would be made of it. This did happen occasionally— Northallerton Prison in Yorkshire had a contract with a local miller for the supply of flour ground by the prisoners. The hours of work on the treadmill were regulated—a man had to work fifteen spells, each of fifteen minutes. The wheel revolved twice a minute and a bell sounded automatically after thirty revolutions. Treadmills were variously used to operate fans which extracted foul air or to draw water. Crank-like machines also drew water (see p. 123). Many of these machines were operated by women.

Transportation, more in the public's gaze, was increasingly questioned. In England people heard how the English convicts could build roads, docks and harbours, and were doing sterling work overseas, even to the extent of building new towns; it was logical to ask why they should not do the same for their own

◀ *fig 48* Prisoners working at the treadmill and others exercising in the third yard of the Vagrants' Prison, Coldbath Fields

fig 49 Caged prisoners on board a transportation ship bound for Botany Bay—late nineteenth century

country. Their brand of engineering was of immense value to England. At the same time, as more of the better class of settlers made their home in Australia, there arose opposition to having neighbours who were the cast-offs of the very society such settlers had chosen to leave. A movement to stop transportation began in Australia, but it was the suffering of the men during those terrible journeys that was causing the most concern. Reports even suggested that hunger had driven some desperate convicts to cannibalism and an enquiry was urgently needed.

Sadly, England's judicial field lacked an effective leader who could set the pace. America, now, was leaping ahead in all aspects of social life, and American treatment of offenders was no exception. In 1835, New York State abolished public executions and in that year, England appointed an inspector of prisons. His name was William Crawford and he was sent to America to study methods there.

His report to parliament upon his return resulted in the establishment of Parkhurst for young offenders. Originally intended for children awaiting transportation, it developed into a model prison based on American ideas of reform rather than punishment, and this coincided with the possibility of an end to transportation to Australia. Another door was about to be closed and the English parliament was asking, 'Now what shall we do with our prisoners?'

6 New Ideas
1840 - 1908

Although the English were trying to emulate the best American prison practice, many American gaols had a long way to go. Charles Dickens visited a penitentiary in Pennsylvania and was appalled at the dreadful punishment and the soul-destroying loneliness of the inmates (see p. 114). The Quakers felt that solitude must cause a prisoner to reflect upon his past and American prisons operated on this logic; the English parliament was impressed by the reports of William Crawford's American visit and ordered work on similar lines to begin at Pentonville.

This began in 1842 when the old Fleet and Marshalsea prisons were demolished. Only six years later, a further fifty-

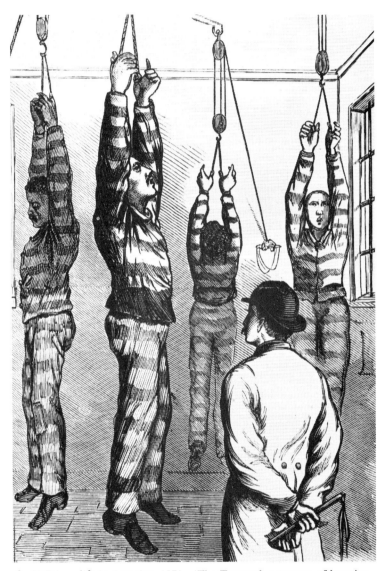

fig 50 Prison life in America, 1871—'The Trapeze', a torture of hanging by the thumbs

four clean and airy prisons had been built on the lines of American gaols. Separation from other prisoners was the aim. Each building had single cells arranged in tiers. They were in separate blocks which met in the centre, something akin to the spokes of a wheel. At chapel or while exercising, prisoners wore masks—a practice which, far from being a reform, drove many prisoners insane. Dickens had recognized the dangers of utter solitude. These new prisons had partly solved the problem of what to do with prisoners who were normally transported. More prisons would solve it completely and in readiness for the end of transportation, many were built. A number of them still exist and are in use—today, they are critically over-crowded and form the subject of bitter criticism by modern day reformers.

In other fields, progress was also being made. Matthew Davenport Hill, the recorder of Birmingham, introduced a practice he had come across twenty years earlier at Warwick-shire Quarter Sessions. Hill followed the example of that early probation system by finding suitable persons with whom to lodge offenders. He believed that, with help, they would reform. Having found a home for them, he made regular checks to see how they were behaving. As with Warwickshire's original idea, Hill had no lawful authority to do this, but he was man enough to make use of, and believe in, his own initiative. Oddly enough, in the same year in Boston, USA, John Augustus, a shoemaker, began to take an interest in offenders, following the day he became surety for a drunkard who was released on bail. When the man went back to court to answer his charge, Augustus went with him to explain that the drunk-ard had tried to behave over the interim period. From this incident, the idea of probation began in America. During the next eighteen years, John Augustus acted as surety for over 2,000 persons. His success rate was high enough to lead to rethinking on the whole subject of American legal sanctions.

Unfortunately, England suffered a minor setback in her

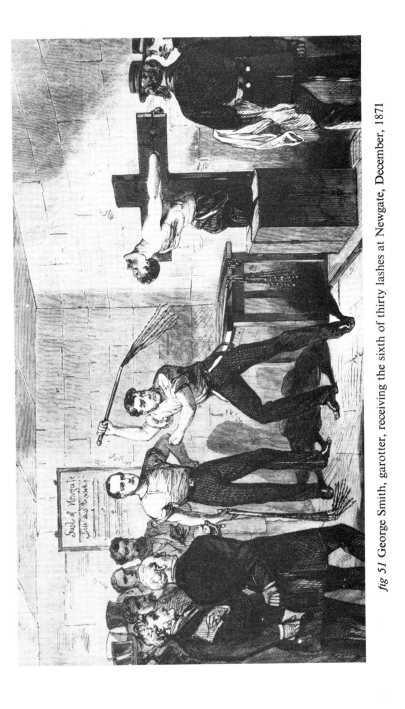

fig 51 George Smith, garotter, receiving the sixth of thirty lashes at Newgate, December, 1871

fig 52 The Hobart town chain

efforts to liberalise. Someone took a shot at Queen Victoria with a pistol and this resulted in the Treason Act 1842 with whipping as its penalty. As another person later shot at Queen Victoria, whipping was felt to be an inadequate deterrent and the Treason Act was strengthened to carry life imprisonment or seven years' transportation, and during the sentence the culprit 'had to be whipped publicly or privately as often and in such manner as the court may order'. Another resort to whipping occurred in 1862 after an outbreak of violent robbery. This was peculiar in that the victims were garrotted (strangled), and such was the alarm caused to the public that parliament passed the Garrotters Act 1863 awarding a penalty of whipping to eradicate the menace.

... of the first efforts

trek home from Van Dieman's Land

Transportation, despite Australia's growing resentment, continued to attract reformers. The current champion, Maconochie, once appointed as governor of the Norfolk Island colony introduced a system which encouraged prisoners to benefit from good work and conduct. By his personal endeavours, a convict could progress during his captivity from the harshest existence to a comparatively pleasant one. Maconochie's ideas proved highly successful, yet they failed to meet with approval. Officialdom said he had gone too far and he was instructed to relinquish his post and return to England. The deputy who took over returned immediately to the old ways and reigned by terror until 1856. It seems, however, that someone back in England had faith in Maconochie, because his theories were introduced to the English prisons. A prisoner could work his way from hard labour (first class) to a stage where he could write letters or even have visitors. It gave the convict an aim in a life which had hitherto been empty and soul-destroying.

Finally, in 1853, transportation ended for British convicts; the government decided to substitute penal servitude, a form of imprisonment. Reformatory schools, designed for the better care and reform of youthful offenders, were established in the following year, and in 1856 the hulks were abolished. Transportation had finally come to an end in England. In France it was to exist for another hundred years, French convicts being taken out to the notorious Devil's Island colony.

British and American governments tried to steer prison life towards reform rather than punishment, but England's new prisons, all full to overflowing, were managed by a body known as the Directors of Convict Prisons. They were approved by the home secretary, but once in office, their ideas were far from modern. Their sole object seems to have been to crush the spirit of the inmates with soul-destroying, useless labour, and their ideals were enforced by individual prison governors who believed a prisoner was there to be punished. One of the activities introduced by the Directors of Convict Prisons was the shot-drill. The object of this—described as 'ingeniously useless' and 'a most peculiar exercise'—was to exhaust the prisoners' excess energy. The event occurred daily from 3.15 pm until 4.30 pm. The participants stood in a three-sided square, three deep and facing each other, their task being to move a pile of large iron balls from the centre of the assembly, round every man in the line-up, and back again. The first man collected a ball from the pile, put it at his feet, lifted it at a signal from the warder, took a step forward towards the next man and passed him the ball. This man put it at his own feet and, at a signal from the warder, picked it up and passed it on. Meanwhile, the first man had collected his second ball, and so it continued, each prisoner heaving 24lb balls of shot from hand

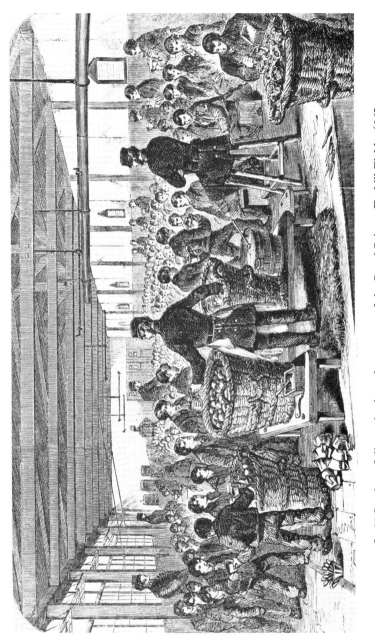

fig 53 Serving of dinner in the oakum room of the Boys' Prison, Tothill Fields, 1862

fig 54 The oakum shed—Clerkenwell

House of Correction, 1874

to hand and placing them on the ground at signals from the warder. As the balls became slippery with perspiration, the men grew weaker.

Another widely practised prison activity was oakum picking. In Tothill Fields Prison over 150 children occupied one room for this task (see p. 119). Oakum picking, separating the fibres of discarded cables or tarred hemp, to be used for caulking the seams of wooden boats, persisted as late as 1939 in some prisons, for in more recent times the material was used on smaller sailing ships and barges. It was considered a useful employment. Each picker had a pile of short, thick lengths of rope or cable. He removed the tar to facilitate the unwinding of the rope into thin strands. Next, he picked out the finer hairs and, eventually, the room was full of floating brown tar dust. The piles of rope grew smaller as the oakum heaps grew larger. When all the rope had been used, the oakum was weighed and despatched. Experienced pickers could quickly finish their quota, whereupon they were allowed to rest (see p. 120).

Prisoners mutilated themselves or tried to commit suicide to escape the drudgery and boredom of their useless way of life. The authorities tried to legislate for improvements, but the Directors of Convict Prisons interpreted the rules in their own way. Food was so poor that prisoners ate frogs or worms, or melted candles into their soup to give it sustenance. By 1878, however, a royal commission did succeed in segregating first offenders from old lags.

By this time the gaols were accommodating the majority of offenders, as other penal methods were decreasing. Gone were the days when the prisons overflowed with suspects awaiting trial, or those in custody for debt; they still overflowed, but it was entirely with men sent there for punishment. A new pattern was forming and even more prison buildings were urgently needed.

In 1874, Wormwood Scrubs was built and three years

afterwards, there began the first major change in prison administration. The Prison Act of 1877 passed the ownership of *every* English prison to the home secretary, whether it contained convicts or merely local prisoners awaiting trial. The cost of maintaining them was to be met from public funds and the responsibility for running them was passed to the prison commissioners. They were to operate under the home

fig 55 Prisoners drawing water—Cold Bath Fields Prison

secretary's authority—the inflexible Directors of Convict Prisons were abolished. The government tried to rid the prisons of the old useless employments, the shot-drill and the tread-mills, and strove to standardise prison labour; but each prison was already committed to its own favourite occupational routines. Some, like Coldbaths, used them all, while Wandsworth specialised in the crank but had no time for the treadmill. The crank was a box-like affair containing sand; fixed to it was a handle and inside were scoops at the end of arms. As the prisoner turned the handle, he scooped up the sand, which exerted a force against his own power. This burned his excess energy—the sole object of the exercise. Each crank had a rev-counter so that a man knew when he was approaching the end of his daily quota. In 1895, thirty-nine treadmills and twenty-nine cranks were still in use; by the turn of the century only thirteen treadmills and five cranks were known to exist, as Home Office pressure was increasingly felt.

The British prisons were full to capacity when in 1866 the government established a select committee to consider abolition of the death penalty for murder. It was not abolished, but *public* executions did cease soon afterwards. The last person to be publicly executed in England was Michael Barrett, who died on 26 May 1868, and the first to be executed in prison was Thomas Wells, hanged at Maidstone on 13 August 1868. This was a small reform, but at least the hanging was swift and sure. The bunglings of the past had almost been eradicated and the 'drop' method had vastly improved from that first tragic use on Earl Ferrers. Even so, mistakes did occur—three unsuccessful attempts were made to execute a man called Lee at Exeter Prison, whereupon his sentence was commuted to life imprisonment.

Norway's last execution occurred in 1875, although it was not then legally abolished, and the following year, in England, the Police Court Mission was established by the Church of England Temperance Society. This organisation quickly found

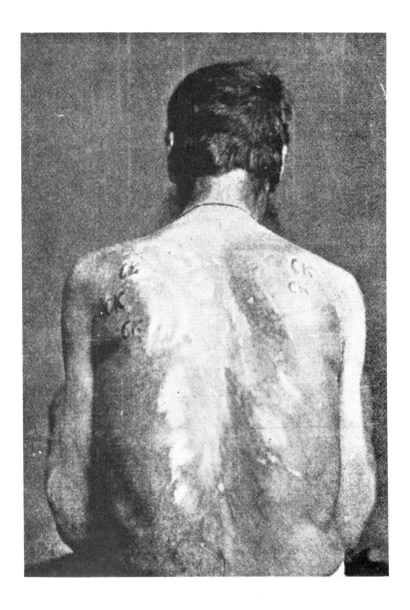

fig 56 In Siberia, each attempt at flight from prison was punished by branding and several strokes of the knout

itself supervising persons on probation or released condition-
ally, or those on bail or a binding-over order. Like many
innovations, this group had no legal backing, but it was
another step towards a complete and professional probation
service, which followed in due course.

In the 1870s, hanging, drawing and quartering was technically possible in England for treason, although it was never
practised at this late stage; the laws had simply never been
amended. Outlawry in civil proceedings was now solemnly
abolished, although it remained a valid sentence in criminal
proceedings. Brutality of punishment was still common round
the world; the Turks were using impalement as a penalty and
oddly enough, this was practised in England to punish the
bodies of persons who committed suicide! France continued
to use the guillotine, although some factions were turning
against it: in 1871, a guillotine was symbolically executed--
smashed and burned in front of a crowd near Voltaire's statue.
On 25 November 1870 the provincial executioners of France
were abolished. The post of executioner was a good one—the
Paris executioner had an income of around £2,640 (a direct
contrast with the Guiana executioners of South America, whose
fee for cutting off a head was a tin of sardines, two bottles of
red wine and ten francs). With no provincial executioners,
France's chief executioner had to travel across the country to
attend all executions. In 1898, however, he resigned, fed up
after despatching over 1,000 victims. In the meantime, Belgium
gave up the death penalty.

Government determination and the spirit of the earlier
reformers were gradually changing things; a reformer, Enrico
Ferri, published a book which pointed out that many executed
men had themselves witnessed executions, and claimed that
many murders were committed on the day of an execution:
brutality bred more brutality, and an execution was not a
true deterrent. Following his reasoning, France reduced her
number of executions and the murder rate dropped. It was a

fig 57 Prisoners were often subjected to monotonous and useless activities

slight drop, but a valid one, and it added weight to Ferri's argument.

By the twentieth century Denmark, Belgium, Holland, Luxembourg, Portugal, Rumania and Italy had abolished the death penalty, but in Paris public executions were still drawing large crowds. During the Paris Exhibition in 1899, Thomas Cook, the British travel agent, organised trips across the Channel which included a visit to an execution. For one particular event he took 280 persons from England—the execution was of two men called Allorto and Sellier, and it drew more spectators than the Eiffel Tower, newly built for the exhibition!

But if public executions were France's shame, England's continued to be her prisons. After being taken over by the home secretary, they did begin to improve, albeit slowly. The Prison Act of 1898 had placed the emphasis upon reform and had introduced remission for good behaviour. This followed the suggestions in the report of the Departmental Committee of Inquiry into Prisons. The act also banned excessive corporal punishment, abolished the crank, treadmill and shot-drill, and sought for the prisoners an ordered and fruitful life. It wanted them to adopt industrious habits and to leave prison better people, mentally, physically and morally. These were high ideals, but those in charge of the prisons did not interpret the new rules as parliament intended. They would not abandon their old accepted methods, so parliament made more rules. The new rules suffered in the same way, always being interpreted to the detriment of the prisoners. As another in the long line of gallant and determined reformers, Ruggles-Brise, came on the scene, he met the age-old official apathy. But in the tradition of his predecessors, Ruggles-Brise was a man of action. By 1902, the hoisting of the prison's black flag after an execution was abolished, and two years later, Ruggles-Brise was sent to America to study the state reformatories. He returned convinced that England could benefit from the

American policy of reform and education. He was certain that this was better than useless punishment and he put his ideas to the test. He chose a village called Borstal, in Kent, where a building was erected to accommodate young men who might otherwise have been sent to prison. Ruggles-Brise wanted them to be improved mentally, physically and morally, and he modelled his establishment on Elmira Reformatory in New

fig 58 The prison yard, Newgate (looking west, 1902)

York State. His schools were named after that Kentish village and today, borstal institutions are producing young men who can take their rightful place in society.

In 1907 England at last recognised the value of the unofficial probation schemes, officially introducing the probationary service by the Probation of Offenders Act. At last a professional service was to become a reality, though the act merely suggested the appointment of probation officers. They were not made compulsory until 1925; meanwhile, the work of supervision was done on a voluntary basis by unpaid helpers.

In 1907 the Court of Criminal Appeal was also established, which gave convicted criminals the right to appeal against either their sentence or their conviction, or sometimes both. Not many years before, there was too little time to appeal: execution followed rapidly after conviction. Since 1907, the right of further appeal has extended to the House of Lords in some cases. The Court of Criminal Appeal disappeared in 1966 and was replaced by the Court of Appeal (Criminal Division), whose functions are virtually the same.

In 1908 the Prevention of Crime Act made the borstal system official and allowed both sexes aged between sixteen and twenty-one to be sent there for terms up to three years. The law *compelled* the English judges to consider the suitability of any sentence, and by this time the possible alternatives included imprisonment, probation, borstal training, corrective training, preventive detention, a fine, conditional discharge or even an absolute discharge. (An absolute discharge is a conviction, but one which inflicts no punishment. It should not be confused with dismissal, which follows a verdict of not guilty.)

It was the creation of the borstal system that led the judiciary to become aware that children and young persons ought not to be treated like adults so far as criminal punishments were concerned. In the previous century, unsuccessful efforts had been made to differentiate between child and adult offenders, and some English magistrates had (unofficially of course) started to separate children from adults in their court hearings. By 1908 this was made law, by the Children Act of that year; it became affectionately known as the Children's Charter and revised the entire law relating to juveniles. In addition to offenders, it covered youngsters with poor home backgrounds, or those in need of care or control. It established children's courts with selected magistrates to deal with all persons under sixteen years of age. Quite suddenly, children were important in legal eyes and it was indeed they who, in 1908, brought about the first breach in England's armour-plated adherence to the death penalty. Capital punishment was abolished for all persons under sixteen years of age.

7 To Hang or Not to Hang?
1909 - 1970

With the abolition of the death penalty for young people under sixteen (later raised to eighteen) in England, came action against the hanging of women. Every female sentenced to death was reprieved, no woman being hanged between 1907 and 1922. As the quest for a more liberal approach gained momentum, corporal punishment was next to be questioned. It was the legal penalty for a host of offences, particularly those committed by young persons. In 1914 the Criminal Justice Administration Act stipulated that no one should be whipped unless the offence specifically carried whipping as the penalty. Common law misdemeanours, which had unspecified penalties, now had to be punished by other means.

fig 59 Child being lashed at school (Note a technique of putting her
on a boy's back and baring her buttocks)

Yet even at this stage corporal punishment was introduced
for new offences in England. The Criminal Law Amendment
Act 1912 specified that offenders guilty of the procurement of
girls for immoral purposes could be whipped, the number of
strokes being left unspecified. This was the last *new* English
offence punishable by the birch; the offences listed in the
Larceny Act 1916 (now repealed) were merely old ones revised
by the new act.

Another long-overdue reform came in 1913, when the
Mental Deficiency Act ruled that the prisons must not accom-
modate people of unsound mind; in 1914 the Criminal Justice
Administration Act already mentioned relaxed the system of

fines, allowing them to be paid over a period of time; it was hoped that these measures would reduce the prison population. Many were serving sentences for non-payment of fines and the space was needed for more serious criminals.

France's long-popular guillotine was still busy; criminals even tattooed themselves with the guillotine as a mark of respect for it, or would tattoo a line round their necks labelled 'slice here' or 'cut along dotted line'. Other countries were less confident of the excellence of their execution methods; in Utah, for example, a condemned man could select his own method of execution—shooting or hanging, as this state did not use the electric chair. Few opted for hanging. The firing squad was formed of volunteer marksmen. Five of them paraded twenty-five feet from the condemned man, and one had a blank cartridge—no one knew who. Upon the order being given, they fired at a heart-shaped target on the chest of the victim. It is recorded that at an execution in 1951 not one bullet hit the target—the condemned man bled to death. Washington suspended its death penalty in 1913; the murder rate rose so rapidly that, by 1919, it was reinstated—but the murder rate was not checked. In 1921 the state of Nevada was experimenting with better methods of execution: the electric chair had been tried, but occasionally three or four attempts were required to despatch a victim; hydro-cyanic gas proved infinitely more certain. In direct contrast to this trend Sweden, in the same year, abolished her death penalty.

By 1921, as concern about punishment was increasing, particularly in America, a visitor reported conditions in their prisons as 'shocking', and told of youths in bare feet, manacled to a pole which reached from the floor to the roof of the cell. A boy could be kept in this fashion for ten days. Witnesses said that warders and governors displayed a lamentable lack of interest in the welfare of the inmates; disgust was heightened in 1936 when over 20,000 people watched a public hanging in Kentucky. But American states were not the only places to

fig 60 Prison life in America, 1871—'The Devil's Shower Bath'.
Brutality such as this continued well into the twentieth century in some
Southern prisons

persist in staging public executions—they were performed in France until 1939. Kentucky abolished them in 1938.

In England, the borstal system was flourishing in spite of the criticisms of the American penal system upon which it was founded, although in 1921 girls in the Aylesbury Borstal were put in irons and there were reports of strait jackets and handcuffs being used on women inmates. By 1930, however, an 'open' borstal was built by inmates at Lowdham Grange, near Nottingham. In 1934 England's first open prison had been founded at New Hall, near Wakefield, and, although there were problems of staffing due to its isolated position, it did prove effective. Similar training methods have since been employed by youth organisations, such as the Outward Bound Trust, to improve physical, mental and moral standards of young people.

While large and important issues were at stake in the penal world, strange out-of-date penalties persisted. In 1938, four people in America were each sentenced to two years' imprisonment for conspiracy to harbour an outlaw, and in England, outlawry was only finally abolished for criminal proceedings by the Administration of Justice (Miscellaneous Provisions) Act 1938. The penalty persisted in Scotland, where anyone who failed to appear at court to stand his trial could technically lose his lands, chattels and protection of the state.

Few European countries used the death penalty by this time. In England, another Select Committee on Capital Punishment had been appointed in 1929. The Belgian minister of justice had been asked for his views and, indeed, many experts from all over the world arrived in London to give evidence. The abolitionist countries were well represented and the committee felt, after a thorough investigation, that *'capital punishment in England could be abolished without endangering life or property, or impairing the security of society'*. The committee went on to suggest a five-year experimental period.

Its report was not even debated!

Behind the scenes, however, the Howard League of Penal Reform was continuing John Howard's work. It had built up dossiers of statistics from Scandinavia which, by 1925, had become almost entirely abolitionist. Even though England officially continued to favour the death penalty, the onset of 1940 saw the number of murderers reprieved exceed those who were hanged. In 1942, Switzerland followed the example of her neighbours and abolished capital punishment. By 1948, the Italians, who had earlier abolished the death penalty, but re-introduced it for certain offences, followed suit. In 1948, too, the English House of Commons voted for a five-year suspension of the death penalty, but the House of Lords defeated the motion and the relevant clauses were deleted from the Criminal Justice Act which came into force in that year.

In 1949 Finland abolished capital punishment, followed by West Germany and, in 1950, by Austria. England stolidly kept hers, but by this time 48.5 per cent of English murderers were reprieved. The lord chief justice of the day, Lord Goddard, was not too pleased by this trend. 'I think', he is reported to have said, 'too many people are being reprieved'. It was in this same year that Sir David Maxwell Fyfe made the famous claim: 'There is no practical possibility of an innocent man being hanged in this country and anyone who thinks otherwise is moving in a realm of fantasy.'

Meanwhile, a Royal Commission on Capital Punishment was sitting in England. It began its work in 1949 and finished in 1953; the witnesses included criminologists with world-wide reputations, from the USA and many European countries. The commission listened to all the familiar arguments for and against the death penalty, but recalled that public opinion favoured its retention. Many citizens felt that hanging was the ideal deterrent to the rising crime rate and, in any case, there was no suitable alternative to capital punishment. Abolition would lead to an increase in the numbers of firearms carried by criminals. As the commission pondered and amassed evidence during those five years, capital punishment was suspended and all murderers were automatically reprieved. This clause was written into the law through the efforts of yet another reformer, Sidney Silverman, whose persistent campaign led eventually to the abolition of the death penalty for murder in England.

The commission of 1949-53 concluded that there was no evidence to suggest the death penalty had any real effect upon the murder rate. In England, during the fifty years prior to the commission, 7,454 murders were known to the police; 2,001 victims were babies under twelve months of age. In that fifty years (1900-49), some 1,210 persons were sentenced to death in England and Wales, but only 632 suffered death.

By comparison, between 1930 and 1950 in America, there were 3,029 executions, of which twenty-one were of women. Most of the executed females were Negroes. In some American state, rape still carries the death penalty, and up to 1950, 809 white men were convicted of that offence. Since 1909, none has been executed for it (though in the same period fifty-four Negroes were executed for rape).

By its thorough researches, the royal commission learned that some persons could never be hanged, simply because of their physical structure. The commission heard that fifteen men were reprieved for this reason alone, because there was no alternative legal method of execution. In 1950 Timothy Evans was hanged for murdering his child. In 1953 John Halliday Christie of 10 Rillington Place, London, was hanged for murdering a number of women; when it was learned that he lived at the same address as the late Timothy Evans, there arose a strong suspicion that Christie might have killed the Evans child. But Evans had been hanged, ironically, almost in the echo of David Maxwell Fyfe's words (p. 137). There was

fig 61 Half-hanged Smith ▶

Todd delin.   Page Sculp.

JOHN SMITH *cut down at* **TYBURN**,
*in consequence of a reprieve which came five Minutes
after he had been turned off.*

a great deal of concern and in the same year, 1953, the Report of the Royal Commission on Capital Punishment (Cmnd 8932) was published. It was regarded as a first-class piece of work, well reasoned and valid, but even as it came off the presses, the capital penalty continued to be a legal punishment in England.

Sidney Silverman rose to the occasion. 1955 saw the last execution of a woman in England. On 13 July 1955, Ruth Ellis, aged twenty-eight, was hanged for shooting her former lover and a month afterwards, the National Campaign for the Abolition of Capital Punishment was founded in England. This added weight to Silverman's efforts to bring an end to the death penalty and as parliament debated over the next thirteen months, all killers were reprieved. In February 1956, all English executions were stopped by granting convicted murderers a reprieve. Silverman had scored another success, but a motion officially to suspend all hangings for a trial period was defeated by 245 votes to 214, a majority of only 31, and executions resumed in July 1957. Between 1949 and 1956, some hundred murderers were executed in England and in 1956 the Archbishop of Canterbury added fuel to the fire by saying that the death penalty was not always unchristian and wrong. There had long been a suggestion that Christians did not object to executions because of their belief in life after death; even if an innocent person was executed, his soul would find peace in heaven. Others had different views—the *Spectator* wrote of 'rustics who regarded abolition in some way a threat to blood sports'.

In America, prison conditions continued to shock thinking people. An American writer of the time, Henry Wiehoffen, commented: 'It is time we Americans realised we have probably the most ferocious penal policy in the whole of the civilised world.' Wiehoffen went on to say that thirty-six jurisdictions, spread across Europe, South America and Asia, had abolished capital punishment by 1957. Of the European countries, only France and Britain retained it, and as Wiehoffen was writing, England was still looking earnestly into the question, in her typically ponderous way. Although there was a need for improvement in the American prisons, the number of American executions was not excessive. Over 7,000 murders a year resulted in little more than 100 executions, but not one American state had abolished the death penalty since 1917. Furthermore, America had no organisation to campaign against it, although one has since arisen.

In 1957, three executions occurred in England, but Sidney Silverman's work was producing results. On 21 March 1957, the Homicide Act 1957 became law and introduced the defence of *diminished responsibility* for murderers. This made murder even harder to prove, and manslaughter much easier. It also created, for the first time in England, a distinction between types of murders: capital murder carried the death penalty and non-capital was to be punished by life imprisonment. Six types of murder were listed as capital: (a) those done in the course or furtherance of theft; (b) any murder by shooting or causing an explosion; (c) any murder done in the course or for

fig 62 A gibbet

the purpose of resisting or avoiding or preventing a lawful arrest, or of effecting or assisting an escape or rescue from legal custody; (d) any murder of a police officer acting in the execution of his duty, or of a person assisting a police officer so acting; (e) any murder by a prisoner of a prison officer in the execution of his duty, or of a person assisting a prison officer so acting, and (f) a repeated murder by the same killer.

Whether by accident or design, the act omitted murder committed during sex crimes, or by poison. If a man murdered someone while stealing a small amount of cash, he could be hanged. If he raped a girl and killed her, he could not be put to death. Nonetheless, the act became law and a few hangings resumed in England. This did not end the restlessness. It certainly did not keep Sidney Silverman quiet for long; no sooner had it been brought into force, than he renewed his campaign. Between the introduction of the act in March 1957 and December 1964, forty-eight persons were sentenced to death in England and Wales, but only twenty-nine were executed. In Silverman's mind, it was twenty-nine too many, and he started all over again to bring about total abolition.

Other forms of punishment were perhaps overshadowed by the hanging debates. In 1958, the First Offenders Act said that a magistrates' court must not pass a sentence of imprisonment on a first offender under twenty-one years of age unless there was no other method of properly dealing with him. But it was not imprisonment that hit the headlines; it was corporal punishment. In 1960, the home secretary of the time, R. A. (later Lord) Butler asked the Advisory Council on the Treatment of Offenders to consider if grounds existed for the re-introduction of corporal punishment. Whipping had been abolished in 1948, but the public expressed a feeling that there was a case for its re-introduction, particularly as violence was becoming such a feature of English crime. The idea was not new—corporal punishment had been used to quell this sort of trouble in the past—so the council set to work. Six years later, it reported that there was no evidence to suggest that whipping was an effective deterrent. Spasmodic demands for a return of corporal punishment have since been made, to no effect.

Sidney Silverman now produced facts to show that while in England a life sentence often expired after fifteen years, the Americans didn't operate their sentences in that way; they gave twenty-eight years or so for first-degree murder and seventeen years on average for second-degree murder. Another feature of the American penal system was that double life sentences were occasionally imposed, eg life plus ninety-nine years. The question of what constituted an English life sentence was considered, for some murderers could be free after eight years, with remission. In 1961 George Blake got forty-two years for espionage; in 1964, some of the notorious 'Train Robbers' were each given thirty years' imprisonment. But these were not statutory sentences; they were imposed under common law. No English act of parliament specifies sentences of such length.

Silverman felt that a life sentence, or the prospect of one, was comparable to execution from a deterrent point of view, but in England, a man serving a life sentence could ask for it to be reviewed by the home secretary and he could even be free after two years. Such 'life' sentences were meaningless. Silverman pestered the authorities with his facts and files until, in 1964, persistence made itself felt. The home secretary said he would reprieve all murderers until a decision had been reached on Silverman's latest bill to abolish the death penalty for murder. In keeping with Silverman's theory, thought would be given to the imposition of suitable prison sentences instead.

On 13 August 1964, Gwynne Owen Evans and Peter Anthony Allen, two Lancastrians in their early twenties, were hanged for the murder of a van driver. They had killed him in the course of theft and were executed in separate prisons. These were England's last judicial hangings.

The Murder (Abolition of Death Penalty) Act was passed

in 1965. This fixed the penalty for murder at life imprisonment. It gave the judge no discretion; if a person was found guilty of murder, he must be sent to prison for life, nothing less. The death penalty for murder in England was effectively abolished —but only for an experimental period. The act was scheduled to expire on 31 July 1970, unless both houses of parliament resolved otherwise. It did not reach that date—under protests from certain quarters, a Labour government pushed the repeal of this act through parliament and hanging was finally abolished. Contrary to popular belief, the act did not entirely abolish the death sentence in England—it still exists for piracy with violence and for treason. (The death penalty for arson in HM dockyards or ships was abolished on 14 October 1971.) It is perhaps for this reason that the Prison Commissioners continued for some time to receive an average of five applications per week for the post of public hangman!

Use of the death penalty was not the only criminal problem to require study. By 1967 over a million and a half people per year in England and Wales were found guilty of some offence, mostly minor, 95 per cent of them being punished by fines. More serious offenders received probation or a conditional discharge, only one-seventh of the total receiving either imprisonment, borstal training or a term in a detention centre; yet the rise in the prison population was as serious as it had been a hundred years earlier. In the 1930s the prison population in England was 10,000; by 1967 it had risen to 35,000 and by 1971 to 40,000. The steepest rise, of 5,000, was in the one year 1969-70. And this growth was in the teeth of a new act specifically introduced to *reduce* the prison population, based on continental ideas of the suspended sentence. Belgium had employed suspended sentences as long ago as 1888, and Poland at the beginning of this century.

The act which failed to live up to the British government's hopes was the Criminal Justice Act 1967, which became effective on 1 January 1968. Among other reforms, it introduced suspended sentences and extended sentences. A *suspended* sentence is a short term of imprisonment which will not be enforced unless the defendant commits further breaches of the law within a given time. The time, known as the 'operational period' of the sentence, can vary according to the court's discretion from between one and three years. If the defendant behaves during that time, the sentence is relinquished. An *extended* sentence, which is little more than a modern variation of preventive detention, is one inflicted upon a hardened criminal who has specified qualifications. It allows a court, in certain circumstances, to extend a sentence for a period longer than that given in the statute against which he has offended.

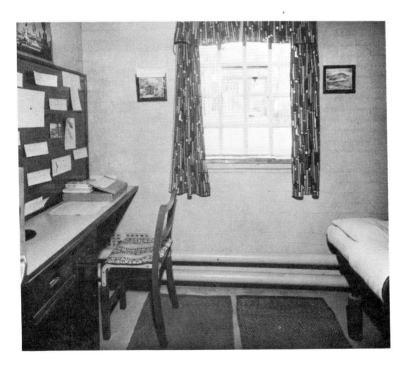

fig 63 A modern prison cell at Blundeston, Suffolk

Suspended sentences seemed easy to administer and the magistrates used them instead of probation, fines or other avenues open to them. The snag was that a person who received a suspended sentence often thought he'd 'got away' with his crime and promptly committed another. This meant he could be made to serve the original sentence (which had been suspended), plus another for his recent crime. He was therefore sent to prison for a term which might otherwise have been avoided and this act, instead of emptying the gaols, was responsible for filling them. This was in direct contravention of the wishes of the Advisory Council on the Treatment of Offenders who, in 1957, pleaded with the courts to consider heavy fines instead of custodial sentences.

Another important legal reform which occurred on 1 January 1968 was the abolition of the distinction between felonies and misdemeanours. The disappearance of those ancient classifications of crime broke the final link with benefit of clergy (see p. 55). Until this date, when a man was convicted of felony, the clerk of the court put these words to him: 'Prisoner at the Bar. Have you anything to say before the sentence of this court is passed on you according to the law?' It was at this moment that a convicted felon of old would quote or read the 'Neck Verse' in his plea for benefit of clergy. But this question will no more be asked and with it has vanished yet another remnant of Britain's medieval laws.

By 31 December 1970, no person under seventeen in England could be sentenced to imprisonment. Those between seventeen and twenty-one could not be sentenced to more than six months unless they had already served six months in borstal, in which case they might be sent to prison for a term between six and eighteen months, but only as a last resort. In England and Wales, the practise is to order suspended sentences for first offenders and the Criminal Justice Act 1967 said that any sentence of less than six months must be suspended, unless the offender had committed certain crimes. In such cases, the courts were given the discretion to suspend such short sentences. In Scotland, no one under twenty-one can be sent to prison unless the court feels there is no suitable alternative.

Most British courts obtain a social enquiry report of offenders over seventeen before they sentence them; persons under seventeen have been subject to this type of enquiry for some time. A social enquiry must be made before a person is sentenced to a term in a detention centre, borstal, two years or less imprisonment, and in the case of any sentence of imprisonment on a woman. So far as young people are concerned, custodial punishment can be given in borstals, detention centres and attendance centres. Approved schools were abolished on 1 January 1971, but the buildings which housed them have remained to accommodate youngsters placed in the care of the local authorities, because of their criminal activities or because of family problems.

8 Summary

Perhaps the most popular penalty over most of the world is the fine. Some statutes specify a maximum amount for a particular offence, whilst others simply allow an unspecified fine with prison as an alternative; the more serious traffic offences carry the latter. But even the fine, as a moderately simple solution, has difficulties. With the court's permission, it can be paid in instalments, and the 1967 Criminal Justice Act allowed claims for non-payment of fines to be contested in the civil courts. But non-payment has reached alarming proportions; in 1970 Britain's unpaid fines were said to amount to well over £5,000,000, Scotland's share of this being about £300,000. Only three years earlier, unpaid fines amounted

fig 64 A general view of Blundeston Prison, Suffolk

to £2,900,000, so the increase can be seen to be rapid.

The fine, now so old-established, is simple, uncomplicated and flexible. It is suitable for all manner of offenders, particularly motorists—who seldom regard their transgressions as 'criminal'. It may be used on offenders guilty of crimes such as minor thefts, but also upon those who use violence or commit sexual offences.

The only restriction in most countries is that a fine should be reasonable and not excessive. 'On-the-spot' fines have been a feature of European traffic regulation for some years and a fixed penalty system for minor traffic offences now operates in most of England.

A case illustrating that the fines system does not always work efficiently occurred in England in 1970 when a prisoner was fined £1 for being drunk and disorderly. He refused to pay and was sent to prison for seven days instead. On arrival at

Gloucester Prison, however, he was found to have £1.25 in his possession, enough to have paid the fine. Acting under regulations, the prison governor abstracted £1 for the unpaid fine and released the man. He had been inside prison for only fifteen minutes, but it was a Saturday. Because the social security offices were closed, the prison authorities were obliged to provide the prisoner with £4.50 for board and lodgings upon his 'release'. So that man left prison with a profit of £3.50!

Currently, the English prisons are once again giving cause for concern, chiefly because of over-crowding, but also due to internal conditions. The problem is widespread in Europe; it has been a feature of America's penal problems for some time and seems almost insoluble. New prisons are built, but are rapidly filled; staffing them is a problem and so is the task of finding useful employment for the inmates.

But America's crime problems seem greatest of all, even though murder, kidnapping and rape all carry the death penalty in one or more of the states. America's last execution (at the time of writing) took place on 2 June 1967. The victim was Luis Jose Monge, executed in Colorado State Penitentiary for killing his wife and three children. Since his death, over 650 prisoners are reported to await the possibility of death in America's prisons. By May 1971, ninety-nine of them were in California; like all others under capital sentence, these had all appealed to the US Supreme Court against their penalty and until that court's decision is known, the executions are stayed. But in February 1972, California abolished the death penalty, the tenth state to do so. The US Supreme Court is to meet in Washington later in 1972 and is expected (at the time of writing) to abolish capital punishment in America on a nationwide basis.

France however keeps her guillotine ready greased, but it has not been used for several years, although some pressure is being exerted to resume the execution of French murderers; the last executioner retired in 1966 and has not been replaced. In

October 1970, a Lebanese court sentenced a man to be hanged and also fined him £10,000 for smuggling hashish. China has the death penalty, too; in October 1970, four men were convicted of torturing and killing three Hong Kong oystermen, for which they were sentenced to death. By this time, Northern Ireland had abolished the death penalty except for two categories of capital murder: the murder of a constable or other person in the service of the Crown, in the course of his duty involving law enforcement; or murder done in the course or furtherance of any seditious conspiracy or of the activities of an unlawful organisation. Russia hit the headlines in December 1970 when she sentenced two Jews to death for their part in the attempted hijacking of an aircraft. This led to a mass protest and also to accusations of Russian anti-Semitism. Their sentences were commuted to life imprisonment. Violent rape carries the death penalty in Russia. In April 1971, Ceylon executed ten rebels and in August that year, Nigeria decreed

fig 65 Grendon Prison—The RC Chapel

that robbery with firearms was a capital offence. In the same month, Syria sentenced five political leaders to death for plotting against the state, and nine Turks were reported to be facing the death sentence for a similar reason.

Canada has suspended her death penalty until the end of 1972, which marks the termination of a five-year experimental period of abolition and as recently as November 1971, a young kitchen porter was sentenced to death by a Jersey (Channel Isles) court. The method was to be hanging, but his sentence was commuted to life imprisonment.

In America, a unique form of punishment still exists; in April 1970, a superior court judge in Fayetteville, North Carolina, made an order outlawing three prisoners who escaped from the Cumberland county gaol. North Carolina is one of a few states where outlawry still exists. Once a man is made an outlaw, he is literally outside legal protection, just as he would have been a thousand years ago in England. Any citizen may try to capture him and furthermore, if he resists the outlaw can be legally killed on the spot. There is a move to abolish this anachronism—a prominent North Carolina lawyer argued that outlawry must be repealed before 'irreparable injustice occurs which could reflect on the dignity of the laws of North Carolina'. As a matter of interest, the three prisoners were peacefully caught within three days (*Time,* 20 April 1970, Vol 95, No 16).

Today, therefore, most of the methods of punishment we know are common to all nations: imprisonment for everyone, including young people, old lags and women; probation, conditional discharge or suspended sentences; fines, mental homes, hospitals and deprivation of privileges, corporal punishment and—in some places—even death.

Occasionally there are demands for absurd punishments —in June 1971 at an Oklahoma court a sentence of a million years' imprisonment was called for against a youth who was accused of raping a great-grandmother—and there are constant demands by the police, the public and the judiciary for tougher penalties. But when they are imposed, they result in criticism and calls for rehabilitation rather than punishment of the criminal, from other sectors of the public. In 1971, the English home secretary forecast community service by convicted persons as part of their 'punishment', an idea which has been considered since the days of transportation when the convicts were found able to construct roads and harbours.

The world over, there is a dearth of new thinking and the problems of old are with us still. The prisons are full and inadequate; they may in themselves be adding to the spread of violence. We still do not know how to stop this canker in our society.

THE END

154 BIBLIOGRAPHY

ANDREWS, W. *Old Time Punishments,* 1890
BABINGTON, A. *The Power to Silence,* 1968
BECCARIA. *An Essay on Crimes and Punishments,* 1767
BRESSLER, F. *Reprieve,* 1965
CHRISTOPHE, R. *The Executioners. A History of the Sanson family, public executioners in France, 1688-1847,* 1961
FITZGERALD, P. J. *Criminal Law and Punishment,* 1962
HALL-WILLIAMS, J. E. *The English Penal System in Transition,* 1970
HART, H. L. A. *Punishment and Responsibility,* 1968
HIBBERT, C. *The Roots of Evil,* 1966
JOHNSON, W. B. *The English Prison Hulks,* 1970
JONES, H. *Crime and the Penal System,* 1962
KERSHAW, A. *A History of the Guillotine,* 1965
KUNKEL, W. *Roman Legal and Constitutional History,* 1966
MAYES, J. B. *Crime and its Treatment,* 1970
PAGE, L. *The Sentence of the Court,* 1948
PETTIFER, E. W. *Punishments of Former Days,* 1947
PUGH, R. B. *Imprisonment in Medieval England,* 1968
TOWNSEND, G. H. *Manual of Dates,* 1867
Treatment of Offenders in Britain (COI Ref. Pamphlet 35), 1968
WEIHOFFEN, H. *The Urge to Punish,* 1957

INDEX

156